Behind the Scenes at
DOWNTON ABBEY

A CARNIVAL FILMS / MASTERPIECE CO-PRODUCTION

Behind the Scenes at
DOWNTON ABBEY

FOREWORD
GARETH NEAME

TEXT
EMMA ROWLEY

PHOTOGRAPHY
NICK BRIGGS

HarperCollins *Publishers*

Contents

Gareth Neame

It was an inauspicious start. As I alighted from my cab outside Drones restaurant in Belgravia (a suitably traditional venue in which to have a working dinner with Julian Fellowes), there he was, hanging about outside, saying, 'we can't eat here, their gas is off'. So began a meandering journey through a London neighbourhood that I suppose the Crawleys might have known well – although of course they were not invented until later that evening. Eventually we found our haven and over a touristic Italian supper I proposed an idea to Julian that became *Downton Abbey*.

I had long thought that the setting of an English country house during the Edwardian era would make a very suitable arena for an episodic television series. I have often been drawn to cinema for ideas, adjusting and fine-tuning them for television, where in place of the one-off spectacle of the silver screen you have a much larger canvas on which to paint all the characters.

'I had seen *Gosford Park*, the movie that Julian had written so beautifully. I had been incredibly impressed by it. It was not so much the over-arching whodunnit element but just the simple depiction of its world that captured me.'

incredibly impressed by it. It was not so much the over-arching whodunnit element but just the simple depiction of its world that captured me. Having worked in British TV drama for a quarter of a century, I was very familiar with maids, footmen and aristocrats, Britain's extraordinary inventory of historic houses and also our literary inspiration for drama. But when I watched *Gosford Park* it struck me how I had never entirely believed in the realisation of the setting in its many previous iterations. For once, I felt comfortable in the hands of the filmmakers and I truly appreciated what a fascinating environment I was being transported into.

Television also offers the joy of repeated pleasure because your audience is able to connect with the characters on a weekly basis. Naturally, some years earlier I had seen *Gosford Park*, the movie that Julian had written so beautifully for the late Robert Altman. I had been

The film stayed in my imagination.

Over dinner Julian and I talked about the DNA of the show – agreeing that it should be equally weighted between the family and its servants. It would have the traditional setting of the Edwardian country house but the density of stories and pace of narrative that is more familiar in a contemporary series. We wanted the show to be something that felt tangible and relevant, so that the audience didn't so much look back nostalgically but could imagine what it would be like to be, say, Mary changing her attire half a dozen times a day to suit the next leisure activity, or Daisy making two dozen fires before dawn. We selected the years just prior to the First World War as the apogee of the country house

and indeed the supremacy of the aristocracy, as much because of the similarities between these characters and ourselves as for the differences. Although their display of rather precise behaviour and manners marks them out as different from us, they have motor cars and electricity, hopes, dreams and ambitions, and are as befuddled by the technology of their age as we are by our latest gadgets from Apple.

Despite our excited and animated conversation about the idea, Julian was initially cautious to revisit the ground he had covered so successfully before (he had, after all, won the Academy Award for his *Gosford Park* screenplay) I think on the grounds that lightning

doesn't strike twice in the same place. However, some days later I received an email, which over no more than a couple of pages described his initial thoughts on all the major characters who would come to inhabit Downton. The inheritance issue, the lack of a suitable male heir, the distant cousin entering their world for the first time were all there from the off. I had a strong sense that Julian had lived with these characters for many years but was only now describing them on the page. At once the world came alive for me.

Julian and I took the project to Laura Mackie and Sally Haynes at ITV, and with their enthusiastic backing I commissioned Julian to write the first episode. I never forget that his opening stage direction set the premise for Downton Abbey in the most economic, but tantalising, way: *The sun is rising behind Downton Abbey, a great and splendid house in a great and splendid park. So secure does it appear, that it seems as if the way of life it represents will last for another thousand years. It won't.* The script was a page-turner and, despite 2009 being a low point as the recession hit the TV industry, Laura and her boss Peter Fincham were so convinced by the material that they ordered the series for production.

Making the first series was a lesson in attention to detail, as we sought to re-enact the style and etiquette of another age and bring to the show the best possible production values that we could. It all went so seamlessly that I became convinced that it was too easy and enjoyable and that the result might end up being a disappointment! After all, so many creative successes have to endure torturous journeys and difficult births. Julian and I had now been joined on the project by our key collaborators, the 'architects' of *Downton Abbey* our producing partners Liz Trubridge and Nigel Marchant, lead director Brian Percival, casting director Jill Trevellick, production designer Donal Woods and costume designer Susannah Buxton.

Alongside Julian's exquisite scripts was the finest cast of British acting talent we could have assembled. What was so satisfying about it was how Jill appeared to

have effortlessly combined much-loved and respected actors such as Dame Maggie Smith, Penelope Wilton, Hugh Bonneville and Jim Carter, with those at the very start of their careers, such as Laura Carmichael and Sophie McShera.

The launch of the show on ITV in September 2010 was a resounding hit and its success was galvanised by a rare spike in ratings for the second episode (very unusually suggesting that all those who sampled the first episode not only came back for more but also brought their friends). Within days of the show's debut, *Downton* seemed to enter the vocabulary and become one of those rare pieces of television that leaps out of the TV screen and becomes a part of popular culture.

We were lucky to have Masterpiece (part of PBS) as our US partner, who have done so much to bring British writing and acting to American audiences. The show premiered in the US in January 2011 to unusually high audiences and it was then rolled out across the world where, in territory after territory (we are now in over 200 worldwide) the Crawleys and their servants seemed to grip everyone's imagination. By the time the second series aired in the UK, with the show recognised as Outstanding Miniseries at the Emmy Awards, it was clear that some sort of global phenomenon was beginning to take shape.

Looking back, it is hard to pinpoint what it was that caused such a sensation. There is seldom only one reason for any creative endeavour of this type to succeed; there can be a multitude of explanations. But I believe a key reason for the success was combining a much-loved, familiar and expressly British genre, that of the English country house, with the pace, energy and accessibility of the most contemporary show.

I also believe that audiences respond to clearly defined 'precincts' (this is why police and hospital dramas are enduringly popular around the world) and a precinct is exactly what *Downton Abbey* is. In every community, human beings organise themselves into hierarchies – in the workplace or at home, we all know our place. We are extremely conscious of these things, irrespective of the country or society in which we live. Nowhere are the peculiarities and eccentricities of social hierarchy more defined than in the British class system of the era we had chosen to depict. So while we all recognise the behaviour, it is a very extreme and exaggerated form of what we have experienced ourselves, and this makes for very compelling drama. Furthermore, Julian's characters can seldom directly express their mood, feelings or intentions. Almost every scene is subtextual to some degree, and again this really gives the viewer something on which to chew. This is a cast of 20 or so core characters – all of them beautifully written and depicted, irrespective of whether the part is large or small

– and because they each keep their own stories running throughout the episodes, they offer unique and individual points of access and appeal to the viewer.

The word 'soap' has occasionally been applied to the show, and despite some people believing this nomenclature hints at a lesser form of drama, it is not a term that has ever bothered Julian and me. If a soap is defined as a weekly drama with an ensemble of characters cohabiting in a specific environment with their myriad personal stories intertwined, then, dramatically speaking, *Downton* is a soap. I would suggest it is a soap of cinematic production values and the finest writing and acting, but a soap nonetheless.

For many people worldwide the Crawleys have become an extension of their own families, which explains the anguish that greeted the loss of beloved characters such as William, Sybil and, most recently and most heartbreakingly of all, Matthew. Although, of course, it is the loss of such characters that not only provides the twists and turns which

audiences have loved, but also provides the opportunity for us to bring in fresh characters, which in turn replenishes and rejuvenates *Downton*'s world.

Downton is unmistakably a drama series, but thanks to the wit of our screenwriter, directors and actors it is also at times extremely funny. You wouldn't describe the show as a comedy, yet humour is so much at the heart of it. Few dramas are as laugh-out-loud funny as *Downton* is. Of course, much of this dimension is in the charge of Maggie Smith, whose bons mots supplied by Julian and whose character's disputes with the likes of Isobel or Martha are frankly delicious, and clearly hark back to what some real people must have thought and said not so very long ago. But although it is Violet's 'zingers'

> '*Downton* is unmistakably a drama series, but thanks to the wit of our screenwriter, directors and actors it is also at times extremely funny.'

that make for the sound bites, there is plenty of comedy going on elsewhere with the rest of the gang (who can forget Molesley's ham-fisted attempts to woo Anna?).

Finally, and I think perhaps most importantly, we have what may almost have been a happy accident of romance. Back at our inaugural dinner, while I knew that love, marriage and the pursuit of these things would be the backbone of the show, just as it is in real life, I had no idea of the dominant effect that this would have on its fortunes. Romance on screen is decidedly unfashionable. We're pretty good at depicting sex and relationships, desire and rejection, but there is almost no role for non-sexualised love. This is consistent with us living in an age with a total absence of subtext, where almost anything can be said and there is little time to be anything other than direct. How satisfying it is then, in an era of extremely complex relationships, of texting and a wide exposure to sex in almost every part of life, to watch the slow burn and simple unravelling of a good old-fashioned romance. Ironically, starved of

such apparently stuffy and staid behaviour, audiences around the world have consumed it hungrily. Fellowes is a master romantic storyteller, but we have also been blessed with the chemistry of Michelle Dockery and Dan Stevens, Jessica Brown Findlay and Allen Leech, and all the others who bring this beguiling element of human nature to life in our show.

It remains to be seen what *Downton*'s legacy will be. Clearly it has reminded us there is still an appetite for a drama that the whole family can sit down to together, something that aside from *Doctor Who* was largely thought of as over. Dozens of spoofs, magazine covers, celebrity (and political!) endorsements and fans have emerged. I also believe it has demonstrated that globalisation can touch many forms of entertainment, for while audiences are in some ways becoming increasingly parochial and favouring their own home-grown dramas, those from any country can have worldwide appeal. Audiences in America do not

feel that this is a foreign show; they want to spend their time with the Crawleys as much as the Brits do. Subsequent series of *Downton* have gone from strength to strength, with the growing momentum seemingly most dynamic in the US, where the show is the highest-rating drama ever played on PBS in its illustrious 40-year history. The finale of series three beat the entire competition across all network television.

The launch of the fourth series felt like the right time to produce a companion book about the making of the show, to offer a deeper insight into how it happens. In their own words, the cast of *Downton Abbey* and our talented crew reveal many of the secrets, previously private experiences and tricks of the trade involved in bringing the show to the screen. It should be a revelatory read for any *Downton* enthusiast, no matter how much you feel you already know about Britain's best-known stately home, the family who live there and the servants who work for them.

Behind the Scripts

Behind the Scripts

The story of *Downton Abbey* began with a dinner and an idea. The idea quickly became a concept for a television series, which was snapped up by ITV. Gareth Neame commissioned Julian Fellowes to write the first episode, and from the opening scene the script caught the imagination of the TV bosses who read it and recognised that they had something special.

ITV is the show's natural home, Fellowes believes. There, he and Neame feel they are better able to present the house's inhabitants as they envisage them, rather than getting mired in the social politics of a century ago, as might be the case at a more 'interventionist' rival.

'When I first read the script I couldn't put it down. I could see each character in my head when I had finished reading. That doesn't happen very often.'

Hugh Bonneville
ROBERT, EARL OF GRANTHAM

'For me, the contention that everything was horrible for everyone except for a few rather unpleasant aristocrats is as untrue as saying everything was marvellous for absolutely everyone,' Fellowes says. 'The truth, as always, lies somewhere between the two.

'We were presenting this very structured, class-conscious society, but at the same time we would deal with all the characters within it with equal weight. We would make an assumption that most of them were trying to live the best lives they could, given the hand they had been dealt. I think that that sense of ordinary, non-heroic characters nevertheless being decent people

who are trying to do their best is the central philosophy of *Downton*,' he adds.

For Fellowes, the world of *Downton Abbey* had begun to take shape in his mind; from the large country house that embodied it to the people who inhabited it, from the major plotlines to the smaller events that they would experience along the way.

In order to create the scripts for this first series, Fellowes carefully mapped out, character by character, a community and the interactions between its members that would tell their story: the rivalry, jealousy, love, hatred, births, marriages and deaths. It was his attention to detail and his vision that has inspired cast and crew alike to become involved in the project.

'When I first read the script I couldn't put it down,' remembers Hugh Bonneville, who went on to play

Robert, Earl of Grantham. 'I could see each character in my head when I had finished reading. That doesn't happen very often.'

For Fellowes, the first character to take on life was Cora, Countess of Grantham. At the time he had been reading *To Marry an English Lord*, a book about the young American heiresses who had flocked to marry into the old English families during the Victorian era, to exchange their parents' newly made wealth for a title and status. 'But what was it like after that?' he asked himself. 'Many of these women were here for years after the way of life they had arrived to preserve had almost become history. What was it like living in a freezing house in Staffordshire which was hideously uncomfortable and far from their roots? The next generation, even the younger sisters of a lot of those women,

would not succumb to the fashion for European titles. The sea receded, leaving these women stranded in an alien culture, with English or Scottish children. So I started to play with that.'

Once he had developed the characters of Cora and her husband, Robert, others began to take shape, each with their own dramatic function. The mysterious new valet Mr Bates provided a spur to the action with his sudden arrival at the house – 'a very simple dramatic catalyst,' says Neame. Anna, then head housemaid, emerged as the show's moral compass, guiding the audience as to how we should view other characters and developments, while remaining far from saccharine. 'When I read

It is the storyline that brings the audience back for more, series after series, and this carefully managed plot is still very much the work of the show's creators, Gareth Neame and Julian Fellowes. Since that first historic dinner, the pair have maintained a strong working partnership, with clearly defined roles in the creation of the show. Together they discuss the storylines and establish a broad overview of where they want to take each series, before Fellowes produces a first draft of every episode. Having started writing for the screen when he was a working actor, Fellowes has trained himself to write wherever he can, which has helped him to shoulder the writing single-handedly.

'All the characters are, to my mind, well rounded and intriguing. There's lots of light and shade to them. They are not one-dimensional and are fascinating to play.'

Phyllis Logan
MRS HUGHES

the first episode, straightaway I fell in love with Anna because I thought she was beautifully written,' actress Joanne Froggatt remembers. 'A really nice person, but not boring,' Phyllis Logan (Mrs Hughes) agrees that for her the characters and their characterisation are an important element of the script's appeal. 'All the characters are, to my mind, well rounded and intriguing. There's lots of light and shade to them. They are not one-dimensional and are fascinating to play.'

The eldest daughter of the house, meanwhile, acted as the focus of its hopes and fears, as she still does. 'You invest in all the characters, but if I had to come down to it, I would say my favourite is Mary,' says Neame. 'The overall dynamic of the show has always been about her future, whether it's the succession issue in the first series, who was going to be the right man for her to marry, or the ups and downs in her relationship with Matthew. And knowing, as I do, where the story goes in the future, she will be at the heart of it.'

'I wasn't really allowed the luxury of, "I must write in this room, I can only write in these hours, I have to have my little [lucky] rabbit there,"' he says. 'That was forbidden me, so I had to work when I had two hours off and I was sitting in my dressing room or in a trailer or in a terrible hotel. I'm grateful for that, because today I can work on a train or stuck in an airport.'

On each draft script, Neame gives his notes – 'what should be accented, what should be held back, "I like this storyline but I think we've missed this key scene"' – and thus they work through the scripts until they are happy with them. It is a surprisingly intimate process for a show that is now so big. 'By the time we finish series four, Julian and I will have discussed, debated and agreed every story in around 40 episodes,' he says. 'A lot of shows have more input from a wide group of people, and in those cases the writer can get stifled by myriad different opinions. This way, I can ensure the stories he wants to tell are brought to the screen.'

Through their partnership, Neame has discovered the sheer breadth of Fellowes' talent as a writer, 'I knew he could bring that world to life like nobody else,' he says. 'A massive part of the show's success has been his extraordinary ability to write romance, hatred, rivalry, love, jealousy, laugh-out-loud humour and tragedy.'

The balance of all these elements within the scripts is delicately judged. 'In a sense, we go for chuckles rather than guffaws,' says Fellowes. 'Once you are making a comedy, you've gone into a different place in people's minds. We have to stop at the threshold.' As he sees it, the humour has to fit with the reality of the people's lives and the characters. 'We have established that Violet, for instance, is quite a witty woman and so we can give her cracks to make without disturbing her re-

ality, because that is who she is. You could say the same for Mrs Patmore. So we've got two women above and below stairs who provide a lot of the humour.'

Certainly, some of their comic lines are now firmly established in popular culture, from Violet's withering 'Don't be defeatist dear, it's very middle class' to Mrs Patmore's complaint that a ringing phone is 'like the cry of a banshee' – just one of her choice phrases.

'She relishes a good line,' says Lesley Nicol, who plays the cook. 'I think she's just one of those women who picks up and connects to language, and uses it. She's got some rather learned phrases. We are all a fan of *contra mundi* [against the world] – we'd never heard that phrase before!' It is this light touch that offers some much-needed relief for the emotion played out on screen.

Among most period dramas, *Downton* stands out in that it is not a literary adaptation, allowing for some

delicious tension around the 'will they, won't they?' romances of Mary and Matthew, Sybil and Branson, Anna and Mr Bates. (These relationships have now been resolved, but these will surely not be the last couples we will see come together on screen.)

A sizeable chunk of the audience seems to suspect that tender feelings linger in the most unlikely of places. 'I enjoy the relationship with Mrs Hughes,' says Jim Carter (Mr Carson). 'And I love the fact that people who watch the programme speculate as to whether there is a romantic link between Carson and Mrs Hughes.' But will they ever get together? 'Everybody wants to dredge up a romance!' says Phyllis Logan. 'I like their relationship the way it is, and I know they are very fond of each other. Who knows what may occur?'

> '**Inevitably there is going to be male interest in this eligible, beautiful young widow. How she reacts to that, how people respond to her and how we see her move on in her life without Matthew is going to be very interesting.**'
>
> **Gareth Neame**
> EXECUTIVE PRODUCER

Romance aside, the show's originality means it can offer up true shocks to the audience - notably the deaths of William, Sybil and Matthew. *Downton's* fourth series opens six months after a car crash claimed the life of Matthew Crawley just as he had become a father. As Matthew's widow, Mary now faces the challenge of building a life for herself and her baby, George.

'That was the hook we left the audience with at the end of series three, with that very long-held shot of her with her newborn baby, not even knowing that she's a widow,' says Neame. 'Inevitably, there is going to be male interest in this eligible, beautiful young widow. How she reacts to that, how people respond to her and how we see her move on in her life without Matthew is going to be very interesting.'

There was a clear decision to reflect the emotional impact of the loss on all members of the family, says

David Evans, who, as lead director for series four, directed its opening episode. 'It was exciting to work on this because it starts so firmly with the household as grief-stricken as they were when Matthew died,' he says. 'I was struck by its emotional honesty. It's the first episode of a new series, but Julian has not flinched from reintroducing us to the characters at their lowest.'

Penelope Wilton (Isobel) was particularly relieved to find this was the case for her character, who has been left grieving for her son. 'The death knocked her sideways, as it would any mother,' she says. 'In a lot of series, when someone dies everyone gets over it immediately. What Julian's done very well is that he's left Mary and myself having a very difficult time, which is much more realistic.'

A shadow has fallen over the whole house. Filming the opening episode, Evans had a note for the cast to remind them to have the loss in mind. 'The advice was to keep the tone sombre,' remembers Ed Speleers (Jimmy). 'Everyone is just a little bit quieter.'

Yet while the tragedy might loom foremost as series four begins, the show remains, as always, a multi-strand story, with a plot that cannot be predicted. Some members of the cast love this unknown element in the development of their character's storylines and deliberately try to avoid getting advance notice of the twists and turns of the plot to come. Others, however, are honest about their desire to uncover spoilers at every opportunity! 'I'm terrible, I want to know everyone's storyline,' Laura Carmichael (Edith) says. 'It's like gossip, "Have you heard what is happening to this character?" But Phyllis doesn't want to know. She's always hushing people if they're reading the scripts on set!'

The show involves a large ensemble of characters, which means that there is always much to learn about those living above and below stairs – for the audience but also for the cast. Even four series in, for some of the actors there are details of the lives of their characters which are still being revealed through each new script. 'I don't know what's around the corner,' says Charles Edwards, returning as Edith's love interest Michael Gregson. 'Very occasionally, you will receive a script for an episode and there's a new piece of information for the character which is a surprise to you. It's rather exciting.' Elizabeth McGovern found the visit of Cora's mother, Martha, played by Hollywood legend Shirley MacLaine, a particular revelation in series three. 'She's a hoofer, a kind of dancer and chorus girl who made good. That taught me a lot about Cora,' she says. 'I was never sure if she was a blueblood American or just the daughter of a very, very rich guy. It became clear to me that Cora's fortune was not one that goes back to the *Mayflower*!'

Even Mr Carson, always correct as butler, was revealed to have had a slightly racier past spent treading the boards. 'It broadens the scope of the character,' says Jim Carter. 'I'm a fixture of the house. Unlike Anna or Thomas, who've had varied love lives and excitement, Carson doesn't have much of that. It was nice to explore.'

Yet there is always an internal logic to the decisions the characters make and the paths they follow. 'When Julian takes a character in a different direction, it's not really a new direction, it's just another layer of onion skin being peeled off,' says Hugh Bonneville. For instance, Michelle Dockery believes that Mary has strengthened before our eyes from 'quite a spoilt, petulant young girl' to a softer, yet stronger woman. At the same time, her character retains her bite. 'Mary still has that incredibly snobbish edge to her,' she says. 'As much as she's grown and become more vulnerable as the series has gone on Julian never leaves out that side of her that's still a bit of a snob. I like seeing that.'

As Lesley Nicol puts it, 'What's nice about Julian's writing is that he has allowed everyone to develop a side of their character that was there to begin with, but which becomes more evident with every series.'

Crucially, it is always easy for the viewer to connect with these people who lived the best part of a century ago. 'Ultimately, the show is about relationships, and a lot of the issues in *Downton* are ones that we face today; somebody falling in love, or falling in love with the wrong person, or experiencing rivalry at work,' says Joanne Froggatt. 'I think the period that it's set in is near enough to our time that it feels familiar to us, as well as being very different. There's a real array of characters too, so there's somebody to love – or to love to hate. It ticks a lot of boxes. It's a period script, but in a very modern way.'

The script, of course, is just words on a page until it is brought to life by these flesh-and-blood people. The hard work to achieve this was over before an episode had ever aired, with the creators working with the casting director, Jill Trevellick, to assemble the cast.

Some parts were decided through straight offers to the more established names, such as Hugh Bonneville and Dame Maggie Smith. 'It was one of those funny things when, for most of the roles that are played by established recognisable actors, we got our first choice,' says Fellowes. 'Maggie signed up, Hugh signed up, Elizabeth signed up and then the momentum was going. We were incredibly lucky.'

As much thought went into casting the junior roles, but the actors were chosen through auditions. 'We spent a few months trying to get the dynamic right between all of them,' says Brian Percival, lead director on the first series. For him, Sophie McShera – attending her audition in a maid-like outfit of a black cardigan with a white lace collar – stood out among the would-be Daisies. 'We'd seen a lot of people and they were fine but they just weren't right,' he says. 'She was fantastic straightaway. And Jo [Froggatt] too. She has all the right qualities for Anna, very sympathetic, but at the same time very beautiful, with an honest and trustworthy feel about the way that she plays the character.'

Since *Downton* is a far from static world, bringing the scripts to life demands a near-constant process of casting as major and minor characters arrive and depart. Unlike American series, which tend to lock in their cast for five or seven years, *Downton* works, as is standard in the UK, on contracts that 'option' (lay claim to) an actor for up to three years. The show has no option on Maggie Smith, notes Fellowes, it being 'entirely up to her whether she wants to continue or not.' For some of the cast the end of series three was the time when they decided to move on – with an explosive impact on the plot in one case. 'As much as we didn't want to lose Dan Stevens [Matthew], ironically his leaving ended up being the best thing that could happen to us in terms of new storylines,' says Neame. 'The scripts are all the stronger for Mary being back at square one again.'

As for finding new cast members, Fellowes and the show's producers have the final say; the producers attend the auditions but film each one so that Fellowes can watch them on DVD later. The director of the relevant episodes also has some input, alongside the casting director. Cara Theobold, playing kitchen maid Ivy, is one of the cast who has most recently been

director will be in pre-production, another in the midst of filming and the third hard at work in the edit suite. Each one may return for future episodes – their own filming schedules allowing – but the producers like the variety, as it adds to the feeling of freshness and energy on set. The first to shoot was Brian Percival, who won an Emmy for his work as lead director on series one and returned to direct on the second and third series.

Of course, as cast and crew gathered together on set, no one knew how the show would be received. The first scene shot was a courtyard chat between Siobhan Finneran and Rob James-Collier, playing scheming servants O'Brien and Thomas – chilly in every way. 'It was minus six on a February morning,' Percival says with a laugh. 'We thought, "Oh well, this is the start of a journey!" It was nothing spectacular or grand; you tend to start with small scenes to get everyone settled in. There's always a nervous energy about first days.'

Throughout the process, he knew it was crucial to pique the viewers' interest. 'I thought if we can keep the audience till the end of the first act – which is about

'My thought was that if we can keep the audience till the end of the
first act, then we've got them… I had to shoot it in a way that would not
let the audience stop for breath or, worse, reach for the remote!'

Brian Percival
DIRECTOR

ten minutes in – then we've got them,' he says. 'So we tried to create a rollercoaster feel and introduced pretty much the whole cast, with the exception of Violet. I had to shoot the episode in a way that would not let the audience stop for breath or, worse, reach for the remote! I hoped they'd be hooked and we'd go from there.'

Now, the show runs like clockwork, and the process of translating scripts into action follows a precise structure. Each series is split into five 'blocks' – the first representing episodes one and two; the second,

through this process, via three auditions during her final year at drama school. 'It was my first professional job,' she says. 'The perfect part happened to be the one that I auditioned for first.' That didn't mean she avoided a nail-biting wait, however. 'I had to go home at Christmas and sit and watch the special on TV. I knew I had a recall, but nothing more. I had no expectations, I just thought it was a good experience. And here I am.'

The new arrivals are not only those in front of the camera; each series boasts multiple directors, as the demands of its timetable mean that at any point one

CLOCKWISE FROM TOP LEFT
Director David Evans (kneeling) plans a shot with director of photography Nigel Willoughby (standing directly on his right). First assistant director Chris Croucher (left) discusses a scene in rehearsal with director Andy Goddard. Director Jeremy Webb explains his vision for a scene during Bates's incarceration in prison. Director David Evans consults his shot list under the light of a prop lantern.

episodes three and four, and so on, with the fifth devoted to the longer Christmas special. Each of these blocks are overseen by individual directors and each takes about five weeks to shoot. Before filming begins, however, David Evans, as lead director for series four, oversees the rehearsals for each block.

Once shooting begins, it is full-on. 'It's a bit like steering an ocean liner,' he says. 'You need to think clearly, because the decisions you make at nine o'clock are still being felt at 3 p.m. So, you might say, "Is it really five camera set-ups?" and you might not be able to shoot the scene that way.'

For a typical scene that is shot, for example, in the library at Highclere, vans packed with light fittings and other equipment are parked by the imposing front doors, but positioned so that they are not visible through the castle's windows.

A couple of minutes' walk from the house, a flurry of activity is underway at the 'base' of trailers parked bumper-to-bumper, housing make-up, wardrobe, dressing rooms and the production office. The cast often jump into a car standing by to drive them the short distance to the set, to spare their costumes and hairstyles from a brisk wind or splash of country mud.

Shooting a scene begins with the cast, still clutching their scripts, being herded on set by the first assistant director for a line run – quite literally a run-through of their lines. This offers a chance for the actors and director to establish how the scene should work.

'They are always looking to find some little detail they haven't been able to do before,' says Evans. 'Actors generally don't come onto the set with the lines off pat and they are not too set in their ways as to how they will do the scene.' The aim is for there to be a sense of creativity, after all. 'I try and learn my lines quite far in advance,' notes Lily James (Rose). 'But some people learn them on the morning in the make-up trailer because they want the scene to be fresh.'

However, the show's script supervisor is always ready to prompt the actors when they are rehearsing

on set – in addition to making sure that the script flows without any continuity issues between scenes, and writing daily notes to keep the show's editor informed of decisions that are made while filming.

The actors build on the director's notes to develop their performances. Ed Speleers, for instance, explains how Evans helped him tap into something that is crucial to his character, Jimmy – 'simply, that the footman is bored. He's always thinking about what's going on outside the house. That's why he's so interested in the girls. At the end of the day, he's just a young bloke who wants to have some fun. Before you know it, you're there.'

The scene is then blocked out, which means establishing the actors' various positions on the set, followed by a 'crew show' for members of the costume, make-up and art department who are on hand to check everything looks right from their perspective. 'Everybody troops into the room and stands round the edges as they talk out the entire thing, almost like it's a little play for the various departments,' says Evans.

The actors then disappear, to be made completely ready for camera in terms of make-up and costumes, while the focus shifts to the director of photography, Nigel Willoughby, overseer of the show's cinematography. 'I'm in charge of the look and the camerawork essentially – so, the lighting, and how we stage scenes,' he explains. Together with the director, he and his two camera operators discuss how the scene will be filmed, and what camera set-ups would work best. Since its start, *Downton* tends to have two cameras filming together, unless it is a wide shot.

Next, it is time for the director, too, to retreat, and the set then belongs to Willoughby, his chief electrician (known as the 'gaffer') and the electricians for the half an hour or so it will take to arrange the lighting exactly as required. The actors are called back to the set for another run-through in front of the cameras before a bell signals for quiet and the first assistant director shouts 'Shooting!' Then he tells the camera operator to roll camera and finally the take will be shot.

Watching the action unfold via a TV monitor will likely be executive producer Liz Trubridge. Having produced the show since its start, she spends much of her time overseeing filming. 'When she's on set it is an extremely comfortable place,' says Evans. 'The person who is basically the guardian of the spirit of *Downton Abbey* on set can be called on if people have questions.'

Indeed, Hugh Bonneville believes it is key that, just as the show enjoys a single authorial voice, it has a similar unity in the way it is run by production company Carnival Films. 'It's produced by a team of people, but it's not ten different producers from five different production companies,' he explains. 'It's one clear vision.'

On a day-to-day level, each producer has different responsibilities in managing their role but they have found a shared rhythm to their work. 'Producing is the most unspecific of all of the jobs in making a show,' Neame explains. Every producer works slightly differently; there's no one way to do it. The nature of the job that you do does depend on the show you're making.'

Neame, the 'custodian of *Downton*', runs the production company, procures the finance from its owners, collaborates with Julian Fellowes on scripts and also approves the casting, editing and post-production work. That leaves Fellowes, who holds the title of executive producer as well as writer, to focus on the scripts, and Trubridge on the ground as the 'nitty-gritty executive producer, working directly with the directors and actors,' says Neame. 'As long as we've got a script that we're happy with, and we've chosen the director we're happy with, I know that Liz will manage all the production side with great creativity, flair and brilliant efficiency.'

Also part of the team are Rupert Ryle-Hodges, who organises the logistics – from when shooting takes place, to how much money is being spent – and Nigel Marchant, who as co-executive producer has a more supervisory role. 'We are the enablers,' Trubridge summarises. 'There isn't a single day that's similar, and that's part of the joy of this job.' A benefit to having reached a fourth series, she laughs, is that now, 'as a team, we know the pitfalls – we know what can and will work and what can't and won't.'

> 'There isn't a single day that's similar, and that's part of the joy of this job. As a team, we know the pitfalls – we know what can and will work and what can't and won't.'
>
> Liz Trubridge
> EXECUTIVE PRODUCER

For all things historical, there is Alastair Bruce, who can often be found on set in the folding chair that bears his affectionate nickname 'The Oracle'. The author of several books, he was recruited after working with Fellowes on projects such as *The Young Victoria*. On *Downton*, attention to historical detail underpins the stories told on screen, he stresses. 'Normally, historical advisors are broadly ignored in projects or at the sideline, but because of how important my role is to the delivery of *Downton Abbey* I sit at the front with Liz Trubridge and we work hand-in-hand.'

Bruce's role, as he sees it, is to help the director to deliver a coherent piece that links to the period – even if the audience is not aware that this is happening. 'Whereas directors normally try to take Julian's written words and turn them into a good performance, delivering it to the conscious side of the viewer, I'm the one who's working in the background trying to make sure that the viewer's subconscious is also satisfied.'

This means that on set Bruce will be constantly monitoring that whatever action the director wants to shoot fits in with the period and, more specifically,

Executive producer Liz Trubridge (left), pictured with Julian Fellowes, brings calm and order to a busy set.

Historical advisor Alastair Bruce is always on hand to ensure every period detail is right.

For the weeks spent filming at Highclere, the grounds beneath the castle become home to the 'travelling circus' of trailers that accompanies the production team.

with what would be happening at that time of day in a house of that size. 'The house is an organism that has a daily structure,' he explains. 'The reason why timings are so important is because you cannot run a house like Downton Abbey without closely watching the very specific schedule, so that everybody's eating at the right hour in order that the house can operate effectively.'

That focus translates into everything from making sure that the costume is coherent with the time of day (not as straightforward as it sounds, since Mr Carson the butler, for instance, would have changed into his eveningwear before Lord Grantham), to what items the servants should be carrying in the background.

The hierarchy, meanwhile, informs everything. 'I got a bit carried away the other day,' Sophie McShera revealed. 'We had the extras in, and I'm really bolshie

Highclere with 70 people asking you questions and Lady Carnarvon flitting round, the next it's just two blokes with a computer, having a mid-morning banana!'

Their task, over roughly a fortnight, is to shape what has been filmed into a coherent whole. The producers will already have been looking at the 'rushes' (what has been filmed) every day and spotting anything that may need to be changed or re-shot – which is rare.

Nonetheless, whole scenes will be cut. The scripts are deliberately written long, so that the action has to be squeezed into the running time, creating pace and energy. 'I like it that way, because then you are genuinely editing something,' says Neame. 'The script is a template, it is not the Bible. So when you go into editing, you're essentially doing another draft of the script. We're asking: "Does the story work without that

'The director's life is amazing. One day you're at Highclere with 70 people asking you questions and Lady Carnarvon flitting around, the next it's two blokes with a computer, having a mid-morning banana!'

David Evans
DIRECTOR

to the kitchen maids – I tell them it's because I'm the sous chef. But I was being a bit bossy with the house-maids, too, and realised they are above me! I checked with Alastair and he said, "The kitchen is your domain, but you can't be too cheeky to them."'

The audience may not consciously be aware of these little accuracies, but added together they help transport us to a different world. 'The viewers feel they are in the space, as they're legitimately seeing the way a house like that would work,' says Bruce.

When filming concludes, the post-production process begins – and if directing an episode has something in common with steering an ocean liner, the director returns to the editing suite with a much smaller crew. 'Just me and Al Morrow [the series editor],' laughs David Evans. 'The director's life is amazing. One day you're at

scene?" or "Can we just have those four lines from the scene and make it much shorter?" It's a fun part of the process. You're going back to the story and you're re-telling it, but this time you're doing it with pictures and performances, rather than with the words on the page.'

It is a team effort, which can produce as many as ten different iterations of the version, or 'cut', from the director and editor, as the producers give their feedback. Whole scenes will be taken out, put back in and switched in order, until Neame, Fellowes and Trubridge are satisfied and it is sent to ITV. Once all the executives involved have signed off the cut, it is 'locked'. Since the edit process has been carried out on a flexible, digitised version of the film, the finished cut has to be reproduced using the original HD footage to produce the final, or 'online', product.

The grading can then take place, whereby the show's colourist Aidan Farrell, at finishing facility The Farm, digitally enhances the images that have been shot. On a practical level he can make day look like night, or a summer shoot appear to have taken place in deep midwinter, if needed – but his role is really about adding further contrast, hue and texture to the footage, to strengthen the mood and atmosphere. Farrell sees this process as the driving factor behind *Downton*'s famously rich feel. 'Going back to series one, at that time period dramas were quite brown, desaturated and old-looking,' he notes. 'We wanted a completely new look for the genre, so we went for really bold colours.' Orchestrating the whole sequence of events is Jess Rundle, the post-production supervisor, who plans the viewings with the executives and makes sure the show comes in on budget and on time.

Finalising the visual aspect of the show is far from the end of this process, however. Just as what is seen on screen is dramatically refined, so is the audio aspect. Each episode is scored with around 20 to 25 minutes of music, made up of some 20 to 30 'cues' – the individual pieces of music that underpin the drama. As a rule, comic scenes tend to use less music, while the more harrowing, emotional storylines demand more. Either way, the score acts as a key storytelling tool, says John Lunn, the Emmy Award-winning composer who has written for the show since its start. 'I'm not trying to conjure up an era in the incidental music, although I'm not ignoring it either,' he explains. 'It's not the function of the music. It is to tell the story and also, in a long-running series where people occasionally miss an episode, the music works as a shorthand, emotionally.'

As his music hinges so much on timings, he only works from the finished edit. He has a team helping with the recordings and orchestrating the music, but he writes it alone, improvising on a keyboard as he watches the action. The final versions are performed by a 35-piece orchestra conducted by Lunn at one of London's iconic music studios: Abbey Road, Angel or Air.

Many themes and motifs recur in various forms. 'The house has a theme, and there are quite a few themes for relationships, rather than specific people,' notes Lunn. 'Anna and Bates get about four or five, as their storyline keeps changing. Then there's another four or five for Matthew and Mary.' Even death does not signal an end to those. In Matthew's absence, Lunn plans to use the music to 'almost suggest his presence' in his grieving family's thoughts.

The most recognisable melody of all of course is the title music, which grew out of the very first episode of the show. It had no title sequence but simply plunged into the action with Bates in a train on his way to his new job at the Abbey. 'You need to write music for an episode or two to get a flavour of what the show is,' Lunn explains. 'I was trying to find the feel of the train, so I came up with the fast, pulsating rhythm, and then you come to the shot of Bates looking out of the window. He has a past that we don't know about and he's very alone, so I came up with this solo piano, single note, which would go over the rhythm of the train.'

As we near the house, about to be thrown into chaos by the loss of the Abbey's heir in the sinking of the *Titanic*, the melody retains its urgency. 'The telegram is going to change everyone's life and so there's a lot of emotion,' says Lunn. 'These are all clues for the audience. Then finally you get the first sight of the house and that's when the chords open out and it becomes elegiac and almost regal. I came to the next piece of music, when the house is waking up, and the same kind of music worked well. The rhythm of the train became the rhythm of the servants bustling about; the house works like a well-oiled machine, like the train.'

In contrast to the background music, the show's source music – meaning that which the characters can hear – is very much of the time. Sometimes Julian Fellowes will suggest songs and sometimes it is Lunn, who for series four has been immersing himself in the music of jazz saxophonist Sidney Bechet and Irving Berlin, the great American songwriter.

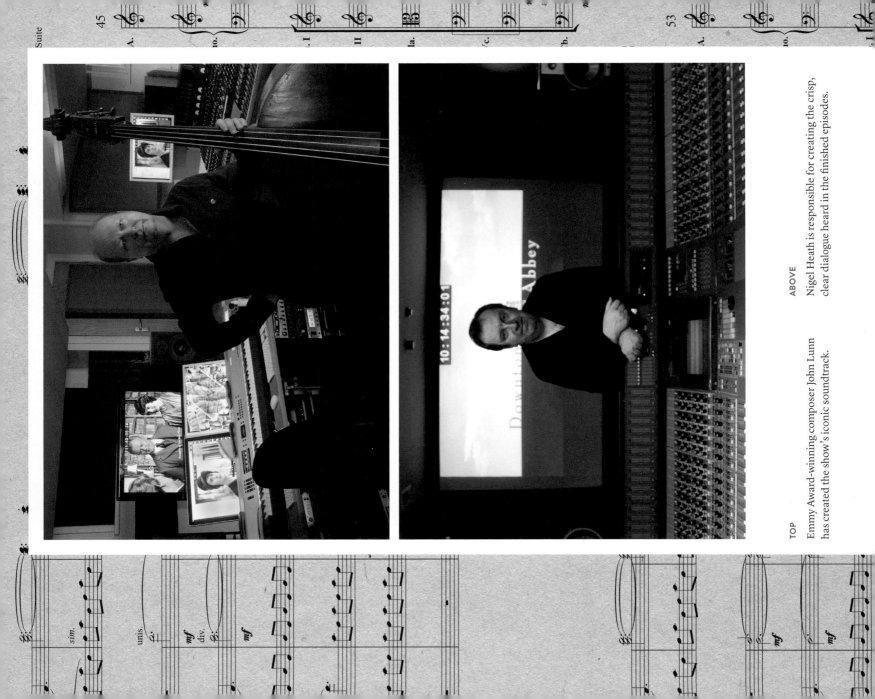

TOP

Emmy Award-winning composer John Lunn has created the show's iconic soundtrack.

ABOVE

Nigel Heath is responsible for creating the crisp, clear dialogue heard in the finished episodes.

On occasion, supplying the source music can mean the show's composer ends up in front of the camera. 'I have got involved in a lot of the music that is filmed on set,' he says. 'At the weddings, that was me playing the organ. Then when Shirley MacLaine sang in the third series, I played the piano for her. I had to wear a wig because my hair is too short, but I'm afraid I hit the cutting-room floor! You can hear me singing on it, though.'

The finished soundtrack, including the music, is woven together by the show's re-recording mixer, Nigel Heath at Hackenbacker, a post-production facility specialising in audio. His starting material is the show's dialogue track, which will have been recorded on set by the sound team, led by sound recordist Alistair Crocker. Their main task is to obtain crisp, clear dialogue. Each performer wears a radio microphone to capture the actor's speech, and in addition the 'boom' track is recorded via a mic held just out of shot. As well as making sure no background sounds leak through – traffic or planes – Crocker also has to silence the set as best he can. For busy kitchen scenes, for instance, small pieces of foam are fixed to crockery, chairs and even the actors' feet to reduce the clamour. 'It's easy to add in the sound of a plate being put on the table, but it's difficult to get rid of it if it's over somebody's dialogue,' he explains.

What is recorded on set is passed to Heath, who with his team carry out the automated dialogue recording (ADR), the process by which some lines are re-recorded – perhaps to obtain a crisper sound, cancelling out some background noise, or to reflect a tweak to the script. For this, actors come to Hackenbacker's main studio in London to perform.

The soundtrack remains far from complete, because everything from the house's hum of activity to the slam of a door, from Branson's footsteps to the rustle of Violet's dress, must be added to produce a sound with more precision and depth than could be captured on set. Much of this takes place in London's Marylebone at a 'Foley stage', in a studio designed to record

footsteps, movements and noises created by props. Here, specialist Foley artists watch the programme on a screen and perform movements in sync with the characters. 'It enables us to access clean recordings of footsteps and clothes that we can introduce into the final mix of the programme,' Heath explains. 'Then we can use those in the show to maybe reinforce a character's mood. For example, if Mrs Hughes spins on her heels and storms off, we can literally make her turn on her heels with the sound; in doing so she wears at her waist can get agitated and we can stomp her off with a degree of attitude. You can build on what the actors are doing to create another level of character. It's very subtle, but it all adds up.'

At other times, Heath will direct the audience's attention – introducing footsteps into a scene so we are primed for the appearance of a character, or making one character's footsteps louder than another's so we focus on her. Silence can also speak volumes, Heath notes. 'You can have someone arrive in a scene without any audible announcement, which means they make more of an impact when the camera comes to them.'

The audio post-production also creates a sense of the house as a character. Here, the team can draw on a bank of hundreds of thousands of pre-recorded noises (including a host that were recorded at Highclere itself) which capture every imaginable crash, bang or whisper that can be elicited from its surfaces.

'Part of the original brief in series one was that the house should be a living and breathing entity,' Heath says. 'The soundtracks on *Downton* are surprisingly complex; there's lots of multilayering going on to reinforce the fact that this is a busy, active house.'

The music track is the last element to be added. As it is a major part of the soundtrack, care is taken so that the sound effects do not intrude on the melody. 'With a sound like Violet's bell, we adjust the pitch of it slightly to make it work with the score,' says Heath.

With all the elements in place, the process of bringing a script to life is complete – until the next episode.

Filming at Highclere Castle

The Home of *Downton Abbey*

For many fans of the show, Highclere Castle *is* Downton Abbey. When the title sequence begins and the huge doors open wide to reveal an English stately home in all its splendour, decorated in the riches of its aristocratic past, we are immediately immersed in the world of the Crawley family.

It may come as a surprise to know that a large proportion of the scenes set at the house are in fact filmed on carefully crafted sets housed in London, at the famous Ealing Studios. Even so, Highclere is an important building, providing a grand exterior and grounds, imposing saloon (the magnificent hall) and the impressive staircase, library, dining and drawing rooms.

Highclere has become a familiar and much-loved location, which has a special kind of magic for both cast and crew. Hugh Bonneville believes that filming at the house has helped him to create his character, Robert, by giving him an insight into the life of an English lord and his role. For him, the stately home offers a 'sense of empire, and of certainty about its place in the countryside'.

The Real Downton Abbey

Julian Fellowes already knew Highclere Castle and had long thought it had tremendous potential as a filming location. In fact, he had tried to use it in the early 1990s for a children's drama he made at the BBC, and later as the setting for *Gosford Park* (although Robert Altman's choice of Wrotham Park proved to be just right for that). Having persuaded the location team to view Highclere, he then had to wait while countless alternatives were visited and tested before the team came to the unanimous opinion that Highclere Castle would be perfect.

The current building has echoes of London's Westminster, which is no coincidence as it is the work of architect Sir Charles Barry, who also designed the Houses of Parliament. In 1838, Henry Herbert, 3rd Earl of Carnarvon, brought in Barry to overhaul his classical Georgian mansion. However, it was not until four decades later that the work was finally complete.

For the show's creators, Highclere was ideal in many ways. Lying on the Hampshire–Berkshire border, it was a practical choice in that it was close to London, but it also brimmed with the aristocratic confidence Downton Abbey needed to embody – even as that Victorian certainty was about to be challenged by the trials of the modern age. In fact, Fellowes calls Highclere an architectural 'trumpet blast'.

Also key was the sense of Highclere being a real home. 'We had to find a house that was still lived in by the family that built it, because we needed their artefacts to tell the story of the Crawleys,' remembers Fellowes. 'When we visited houses that had been bought by somebody else in 1973, the story wasn't there on the walls, it wasn't there in the furniture.' As it is, the Herbert ancestors play the part of the Crawleys as they look down from the walls.

Looking After Locations

Over the last four years, filming has become woven into the fabric of life at Highclere. A typical filming day will see the rooms that are used for the show packed with cast and crew, TV monitors and folding chairs, all arranged over a rubber sheet that protects the ancient floors.

The art department make wide use of the house's treasures, many of which would be impossible to hire. Meals taken in the dining room, for instance, are shot under a towering portrait of Charles I on horseback by Van Dyck. As well as paintings and wall hangings, much of the furniture seen on screen belongs to Highclere, including the dining room's vast expanding table.

But although the house appears to be a ready-made set, some concessions must be made to safeguard its treasures. Although it would have been customary to have only tablemats, the antique dining table is protected by white tablecloths. If there are 18 diners to be seated, these tablecloths have to span the table at its longest – around 50 feet. The snowy covering also has the added advantage of bouncing light off the actors' faces, which softens the look on screen.

At Home On Location

On arrival at Highclere the team are greeted by a bloodthirsty doorknocker on the castle's double doors – the head of a wolf, its jaws filled with some unfortunate's leg.

When the doors swing open to reveal the impressive sky-lit hall, however, the atmosphere suddenly becomes rather warmer. The grandeur of the Gothic-inspired great hall is matched by a sense of intimacy, reflected in the owner's approach to the cast and crew.

In spring, as they begin six months of shooting, there is a notice pinned up inside the doors to inform the team that Lady Carnarvon has offered to take them to see the lambing that afternoon if they would like to go.

It is still very much a working estate. Lisa Heathcote, the food economist, notes a memorable encounter with locals as she worked in her catering tent. 'A member of the Highclere staff was walking the hunt puppies and the dogs came galloping up. They disappeared down the lawn with half a piece of beef and even the parsley. I just laughed! There were a lot of them.'

Precision Planning

A show the size of *Downton* needs to run like clockwork to get through the pages of script that must be filmed each day. Everyone relies on the daily call sheet, written by second assistant director Danielle Bennett. This sets out exactly when each actor must arrive at the studio or location, when they must go through make-up and costume, and takes into account the time needed to travel from base to set.

The unit call time – when cast and crew must be on set ready to film – may be for 8.30 a.m., as for Mary and Matthew's wedding, but for many work starts hours earlier than that so they can be prepped and ready for that deadline. The call sheet also details everything from when the sandwiches arrive to who's looking after the horse.

The longer-term shooting schedule (planning what is shot when) is masterminded by first assistant director Chris Croucher.

'In series four I had one day to shoot scenes with three directors in the Crawley House interior – it seemed better to make a day of it,' he explains.

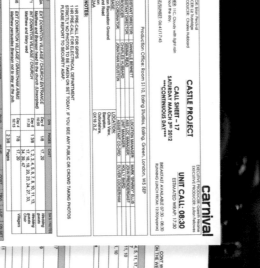

'The sofa in the drawing room belongs to Highclere, but we brought in tapestries and eighteenth-century chairs, as well as some green button-backed chairs. We dress the room with flowers, pictures, framed photos and our china – understandably the Carnarvons put their china away so it doesn't get knocked.'

Gina Cromwell
SET DECORATOR

The Library

In many ways the library is the heart of the house. A less formal setting than the drawing room, it has a masculine feel, as befits the de facto office of the master of the estate. Here, Robert can often be found at his desk with his dog Isis by his side, while someone slips in to browse the 5,000-plus books lining the shelves.

But with its plush red-velvet sofas – Highclere's own – and roaring fire, it is also a room where the family frequently gather to talk, or to have a cosy cup of tea.

'Every generation gets one room more right than others, and the Victorians perfected the library,' says Julian Fellowes. 'No Georgian library comes close to a marvellous early-Victorian library, and I think Highclere has one of the most beautiful in the country. To film there every day is a real privilege.'

As an actor, Hugh Bonneville is also a fan of working within its walls, for more practical reasons. 'I think my favourite room to film in is the library, because it's so big. There's so much variety in it, and a feeling of space.'

A World of Bustle and Calm

The world of the servants is one that is far removed from that of the family they serve. There is an opulence to the life above stairs, which is deliberately emphasised through the design of the sets and the style of filming to show the contrast with the servants' more rough-and-ready existence.

'The below-stairs sets created at Ealing are very grey, slightly colourless – reflective of their lives,' says Charmian Adams, the art director. 'And then, once you open that green baize door and they move from their lives into the life above stairs, filmed at Highclere, everything is suddenly more colourful, more vibrant and glossy. The furniture is polished, it's all beautiful – the people are beautiful, and their clothes are beautiful, and they have everything done for them.

'The servants work like mad; it is like a factory underneath the house, where they are polishing, scrubbing and cleaning to maintain the serenity upstairs.

Obviously Downton has its ups and downs – people die, all sorts of awful things happen – but visually it appears to be a calm and elegant place.'

The pace of the family's movements above stairs reflects this too, and their rooms are at their busiest only when the maids and footmen almost imperceptibly go about their business. The footmen stand quietly to hand, unnoticed until they are needed, particularly at dinner, but the housemaids whirl round the ground-floor rooms and bedrooms at speed. Alastair Bruce, historical advisor for the show, reminds us that this speed is important, because maids were expected to do their work surreptitiously, out of sight of the family. 'Women worked extremely hard to keep those houses going, but they were never allowed to be seen. They came and did their work, but never when the family were around. They would be invisibly puffing up pillows, cleaning, polishing and scrubbing.'

FLEETS OF FOOTMEN

According to Alastair Bruce, Highclere Castle would have been staffed by many more footmen than Downton's Alfred and Jimmy. 'You couldn't have run a house of that size with so few footmen – there would have been probably seven or nine ... but we're making a drama. If you started to try and cast seven footmen, it would be the footmen show.'

THE SHOW GOES ON

As Jim Carter (Mr Carson) puts it, 'Below stairs is backstage and it's our job to make sure that above stairs it is a perfect stage performance. The servants exist sort of in the shadows and we are fairly invisible to the family.'

'As you come down the drive and this great sculptural mass is sitting there with its pinnacles and towers, you see why Robert feels that whatever happens he's got to keep the house going. He has to hand it on; he can't be the one who drops the baton.'

Julian Fellowes
EXECUTIVE PRODUCER

Anyone for Cricket?

For the summer game of cricket, which pits the Abbey against the village, Highclere Castle offered its very own pitch and pavilion. However, shooting outdoors left the cast and crew at the mercy of the British weather. 'That summer was wet all the time', remembers executive producer Liz Trubridge. 'We really were worried that we weren't going to be able to do it, and Highclere, understandably, didn't want us to go on their pitch if it was sodden because it could make a huge mess.' So the team hired a 'blotter' – like those used at international cricket grounds – to soak up the puddles.

There was still the threat of more rain, however. 'On the way down there was the most terrific downpour,' says Trubridge. 'I thought, "How are we ever going to get this sequence?"' But the gods were smiling. 'When we got to Highclere, blue sky appeared! They hadn't had the downpour there and we filmed for three days in dry weather. Then about two hours after we wrapped, it started to rain and it didn't stop raining for days.'

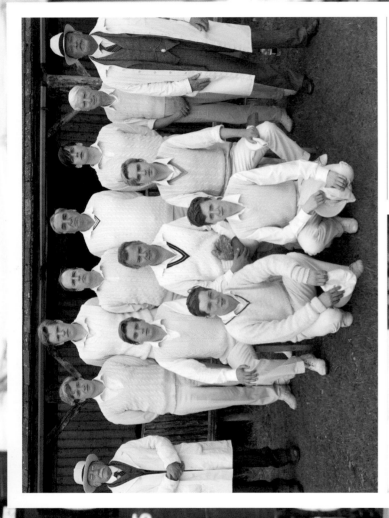

PLAYING AGAINST THE WEATHER

The sun might have shone on Downton's cricketers, but the weather has not been so kind for other outdoor scenes. When shooting scenes in the gardens of the country house to which the Crawley family thought they might have to 'downsize', bad weather forced the production team to change their planned filming dates three times.

FAMILY TIES

As she cradles her niece, baby Sybbie, in this idyllic English scene, Mary has no idea that these breezy, happy summer days with husband Matthew are soon to end. After Mary is widowed, Tom tries to help her through her grief, says Michelle Dockery (Mary). 'Tom tries to bring her round because they have something in common – they've both lost their partners and are left with young babies.'

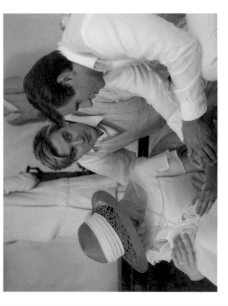

Filming at Ealing Studios

The Set Divide

As the butler, Jim Carter plays one of the characters who can move fluidly between the two worlds at Downton Abbey, but as an actor he does admit to a personal preference in terms of locations. 'Highclere is essentially opening doors, "dinner is served" and standing watching posh people eat breakfast,' he sums up. 'For me, the scenes in my office, or my pantry as they call it, are more fun.' Phyllis Logan (Mrs Hughes) agrees: 'I do like it when Mr Carson and Mrs Hughes do a round-up in either her sitting room or his pantry with a glass of sherry.'

For the below-stairs cast, Ealing is a more familiar location; many of these actors rarely visit Highclere, because their characters make only occasional trips through the green baize door. For example, Mrs Patmore, as the cook, would have had no reason to go

into the family's rooms. 'I have been a few times,' says Lesley Nicol, 'but it has to be a big event where the servants are all together ... a wedding or a funeral!' Cara Theobold (Ivy) films mostly at Ealing, and her rare scenes at Highclere generally take place in the kitchen courtyard. 'I've been in the great hall and stoked some fires, but Ivy would never be in the family rooms – or any room that an above-stairs character would be in.'

The actors don't mind, because Ealing offers a more intimate environment. Ed Speleers (Jimmy) remarks, 'It's lovely to go to Highclere; it's a beautiful place to go to get away from the hubbub of London, but I prefer working at Ealing. I love the old English studios. Highclere is more of a training ground for me – I get to watch what's going on. But Ealing is where all my nuts and bolts take place.'

Building Below Stairs

The below-stairs rooms dominate the *Downton* stage at Ealing Studios, simply because, as with many stately homes, they no longer exist at Highclere in their original state.

The silver lining to that problem was that the show's designers could create what they needed. In this way every room in the servants' quarters could be meticulously designed for historical accuracy, but also to accommodate a large cast, crew and their equipment.

The result is a fixed, interlocking structure that includes the kitchen complex, the servants' hall, Mr Carson's pantry, Mrs Hughes's sitting room and now a boot room – as well as stairs that appear to lead up to the family's part of the house. Donal Woods, the production designer, cites the hit US political drama *The West Wing* as a surprising inspiration for the set, which boasts corridors wide enough to allow the staff to rush past each other while cameras swing about. 'It's a similar situation, where you've got lots of rooms,' he says. 'The set was designed for flow and movement, as below stairs is busy and hectic – the characters are in and out. I'm quite proud of this set; it works very well.'

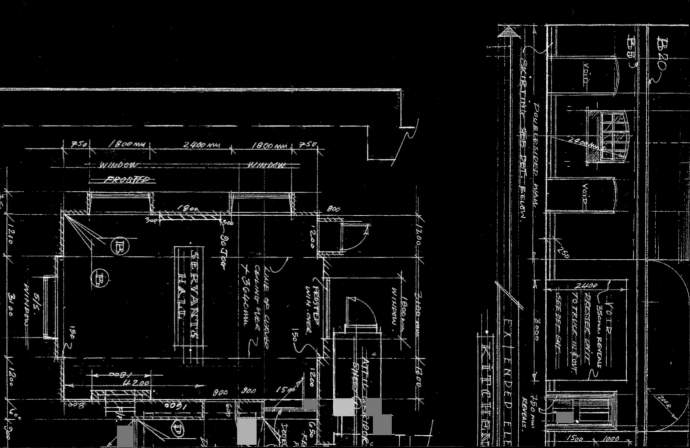

LIGHT IN THE SHADOWS

The house above stairs may be flooded with sunshine, but below stairs the servants rely on electric lights to illuminate their workplace. 'The lights are on all the time because it's under ground – it's dark', says Donal Woods, the production designer, pictured above.

FAMILIARITY BREEDS CONTENTMENT

To Cara Theobold (left), the below-stairs set looked very familiar when she joined the show in series three. 'I'd seen it so many times on the TV!' she says, 'so it was exciting to see it close up. It's such a brilliant, detailed set that you immediately feel you've stepped into the servants' world.'

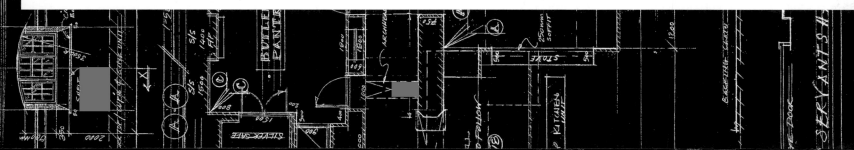

Inside the Servants' Quarters

Wandering onto the below-stairs set in between takes, it is easy to believe you are in the kitchen of a grand country house. You feel that at any moment Mrs Patmore will walk in and start barking orders at you. The solidity of the structure helps to create this realism. The floors are paved with stone flags and the corridors, unlike the other rooms in the set which have open ceilings for lights and cameras, are finished with low arches overhead.

Despite its adaptations for filming, the set retains the intimacy of a working country house, says Ed Speleers. 'I love how claustrophobic it is, especially when we are all there. When you put 15 cast in the servants' hall with two cameras and sound men, you soon run out of room.'

Cameras often follow a servant through the set, which demands technical delicacy, notes Nigel Willoughby, director of photography: 'Setting up the action takes a lot of time, and it can be challenging to light. But if you light everything from outside the set, and you're not afraid to let people walk through dark areas, it works.'

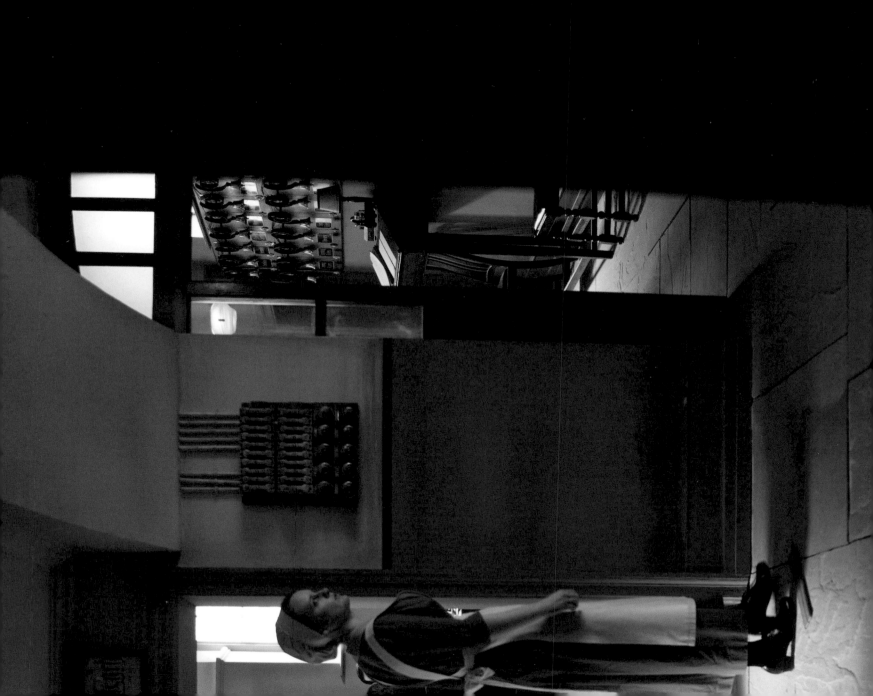

Lights, Camera, Action!

Lighting and camerawork, key to creating the lush *Downton* look on screen, are elements that are overseen by the director of photography, who for much of series four is Nigel Willoughby.

'Every room in reality is different; they have different colours, tones and textures, so I follow that principle on set,' he explains. He doesn't want the audience to see his work, though, because 'the less you notice lighting, the better it is. It's the same with camerawork.'

While Willoughby has his opinions on what makes the best angles and shots, 'it's a collaboration between me and the director and the camera operator. We pool ideas and together we come up with the best solution.'

The look for series four is 'even more luscious', with greater contrast and gloss, he promises. Technically, that means pushing light sources out to the edges of the set. 'We have big lights outside the windows, and in the wide shots that's all there is; there are no lamps on set. This year the lighting is designed to look even more cinematic.'

Jimmy and Ivy use the new boot room for another, less professional purpose than looking after the family's footwear. As two corners of the 'love square', as Cara Theobold puts it ('Daisy loves Alfred, Alfred loves Ivy and Ivy loves Jimmy'), they secretly meet here. There is no question what Ivy wants, laughs Theobold. 'Jimmy's so daring and adventurous, really charming – this is the most exciting thing going on for her.'

SPIT AND POLISH

The boot room is very much a working space, kitted out with every item needed to bring the family's dirty footwear to a gleaming finish – shoe brushes, oils and polishes, as well as a sink – and dressed with pairs of leather boots in various states of cleanliness.

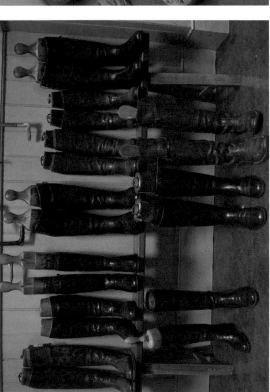

The Boot Room

Like any stately home, Downton Abbey is full of nooks and crannies. Happily for the production team, that means they can introduce new rooms if the plot so demands, such as the boot room, which makes its first appearance in series four.

To create each new set, Donal Woods initially draws it on paper, then he makes a little cardboard model of the design, which he talks through with the construction team. Once the design has been agreed, the team will hammer and saw away to build the structure at Ealing. The lighting department are also consulted, because it is they who will decide how to light the set. 'I talk with the director of photography and he might say, "Can this window be a little bigger?" so it is very much

a collaboration,' says Woods. 'All in all, building a set takes a week or two from us agreeing a drawing.'

The props department, meanwhile, are busy sourcing items to dress the set, such as the worn leather riding boots, shoe polish and brushes. As always, Alastair Bruce is on the alert for anything incongruous. 'To me, everything must be practical,' says Bruce, 'If there are items positioned in working areas that are there to make them look pretty, then that's not right. The rooms are not display cases – they must be practical.' Nevertheless, as well as being functional, the boot room also provides a discreet corner where the staff can share a private word – while keeping an ear out for the approach of Mr Carson or Mrs Hughes, of course.

The Servants' Hall

The servants' hall is dominated by a board of gleaming bells. Their ring is the cue for a footman or ladies' maid to attend to a member of the family in one of the house's many impressively named rooms, such as 'Grantham', 'Stanhope' or 'East Anglia'. During filming, a crew member stands on the other side of the wall, pulling hidden strings to sound the required bell.

For the cast, this set frequently signals a big group scene, as this is also where their characters gather to eat. Often lengthy to film, these scenes offer a chance for the actors to catch up between takes. 'The servants' hall scenes are really fun to do,' says Joanne Froggatt (Anna). 'We have quite a giggle.'

There is another chance for gossip just out of sight of the camera. 'A lot of the time when we do those big scenes in the servants' hall, if we are going to be needed five or ten minutes later they have what they call a herding area for us just off the set,' says Phyllis Logan. 'They put chairs out and we all congregate there and just chat between ourselves.'

'I always remember Liz Trubridge saying to me in the first week that as she watched us on the monitor it was like we'd been here for years. They were ecstatic that we all bonded so well, because it creates a realistic chemistry on screen.'

Rob James-Collier
THOMAS BARROW

The Kitchen

Historically the kitchen was the busiest room in a house the size of Downton Abbey. Out of it would come eight meals a day for the family and servants, not to mention any extra food required for guests.

The design of this part of the set was influenced by the kitchens in old English country houses. Using a kitchen in a real stately home was not an option, because even the unmodernised ones have low ceilings and a general gloom, which makes filming a challenge.

Painstakingly recreated, the set is realistic, featuring running taps, but is also designed with filming in mind. For instance, the tiling behind the stove can be removed to allow cameras to shoot through the wall, to show the flurry of activity over pots and pans. However, only 'a couple of the hobs work and it is just steam that comes out of the ovens', notes Lesley Nicol (Mrs Patmore). Steam often comes out of Mrs Patmore's ears, too. 'If anything goes wrong it's a disaster,' says Nicol. 'She's not a bully, she just has high standards, like many chefs.'

WEIGHTS AND MEASURES

Playing the cook, Lesley Nicol does more directing and overseeing than wielding the pots and pans herself – for which she is thankful. 'They are really heavy, even when there's nothing in them. I'm quite lucky, because I have my staff! Poor old Sophie McShera [Daisy] ends up carting them around.'

COOKING UP A STORM

The kitchen is stocked with all the period equipment servants would need to produce the food served in dining scenes. Lisa Heathcote, the show's food economist, prepares these dishes but also devises tasks for kitchen scenes – for example, deliberately leaving a pastry case unfinished so a maid can be shown adding the final tweaks. 'We have six people working in the kitchen, so one can be putting the cherries on a dessert, another could be putting leaves on a pie.'

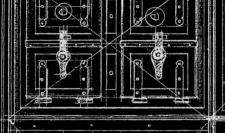

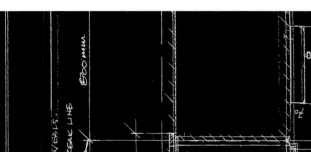

Beautiful Boudoirs

When *Downton* began, bedroom scenes were filmed at Highclere, but the limited space once cast, crew and cameras were in the room made filming difficult. Now these scenes are shot on sets at Ealing. 'We realised that, because we can just take a wall out in the studio, you can have all the crew in a room and we suddenly have a lot more space to work in,' says John Prendergast, assistant location manager.

Space constraints on the stage mean it is not practical to keep every set up in situ for the entire period of filming. The kitchen complex does remain in place, but alongside it there is a constant flurry of set-building, painting, set-dressing and finally dismantling going on. Robert's dressing room doubles as the nursery or Tom Branson's bedroom, for instance, while Cora's bedroom is first transformed into Edith's and then

Mary's. The walls are movable, so their positions and even those of the rooms' windows change, with the construction department all the while referring to their technical drawings of the sets for consistency throughout a series. If necessary, a set can be transformed into another room overnight.

Props add a personal touch. Positioned around the room will be whatever book Mary might be reading – a small volume of Tennyson, for instance. 'This year I've noticed that on set – not just in my bedroom, but in the library, too – there are pictures of Matthew and Mary's wedding around and little reminders of him,' says actress Michelle Dockery. 'There's also one of Dan [Stevens], as Matthew, on my dressing table. That is what is so wonderful about this show; in every department the attention to detail is phenomenal.'

Changing Rooms

With some of the Ealing sets in constant flux, careful planning is required to ensure they are ready for filming when it is scheduled. Everything has to be arranged so that the props can be unpacked and placed on a set that has been painted and decorated, ready for action. Meanwhile set-building has to be timed so that it takes place when shooting is at Highclere, explains art director Charmian Adams, 'because painters and, in particular, carpenters make a lot of noise.'

For practicality's sake, scenes from more than one episode will be filmed while each different set is standing, in order to minimise the number of room changes required. Nonetheless, Mark Kebby, the supervising art director, notes that the walls are repainted so often they are getting 'thicker and thicker'.

Much of the set is reused, so a lone wall panel that formed part of Mary's bedroom – painted its signature green – might reappear in another set, such as Cora's rather larger bedroom, and perhaps painted blue.

Filming on Location

ENTERTAINING THE MASSES

Downton needs locations to suit every part of the Abbey's world, but the three-strong locations team must also consider the movements of cast and crew in their decisions. Normally this adds up to 80–90 people, 'except for big days', says assistant location manager John Prendergast. 'We may have 50 or 60 extras, so then we need 20 or so more make-up artists. Some days there are 150 or 160 people on set.'

TRAVELLING CIRCUS

This emotional scene, as ruined housemaid Ethel agonised over the decision of whether to give up her son to his grandparents, was filmed with quite an audience. Viewers may not realise 'the size and scale of the circus that comes around behind us', says Prendergast. 'We have great fun with it, we really do.'

Scouting for the Perfect Setting

Every series sees new locations added to those familiar to the audience, as storylines take the family and their servants out of Downton Abbey. The search for these properties is led by Mark 'Sparky' Ellis, the location manager, in conjunction with production designer Donal Woods.

They draw on industry guides and recommendations from agencies who specialise in finding locations. For convenience, the team prefer settings not far from the existing ones, and ideally as close as possible to London to avoid overnight stays for cast and crew. But that is just the start of their considerations – the building must also work in filming terms.

'With a show this big not only must the location look ideal, but we must be able to support it', says Ellis. 'You may find a fantastic restaurant in some back alley, but to service it you've got to park about 20 trucks nearby. The last thing you want to do is change your plans because you've found a great place to film but you can't get any of the equipment to it.'

LINCOLN CASTLE

York Prison

Lincoln Castle made a forbidding York Prison, where Bates served time for the murder of his wife. For hundreds of years the fortress was used as the city's jail, with prisoners executed on its ramparts. Lincoln itself was a lovely place to film, according to Joanne Froggatt. 'Being in the castle added weight to those scenes, rather than being on sets. It was really beautiful up there, too.'

As usual, filming did not run in story sequence, but was planned to make the most of the location in as little time as possible, notes Chris Croucher. 'Lincoln, for Bates, was used for six different episodes, so over two days we had four different directors shooting their prison scenes there,' he says.

Those scenes, of course, told one of *Downton*'s darker storylines, as Bates and Anna fought against a miscarriage of justice and the threat of the hangman. For the actors such highly charged scenes can be draining, says Froggatt. 'If you have a few days in a row of emotional scenes you can't help but take it home.'

Hills, Hunting and High Roads

The show relocated lock, stock and barrel to west Scotland for the final episode of series three, when the Crawley family visited warring relatives at Duneagle Castle.

Inveraray Castle, the ancestral home of the Duke of Argyll, was the perfect location, boasting an extravagant state dining room and a vast armoury hall.

For the crew, shooting in the surrounding Highland landscape proved the biggest hurdle, which they solved by using 4x4s to carry the necessary equipment to the locations from bases lower down. 'We were really high up in the glens, with hardly any road,' says 'Sparky' Ellis. 'It was a real logistical challenge.'

Yet both cast and crew speak fondly of time spent shooting on locations further afield, which offers everyone a chance to socialise outside of work. 'The week up in Scotland was great,' says Charles Edwards (Gregson). 'The scenery was gorgeous, and we were all staying in the same hotel, so after shooting we would congregate in the hotel bar.'

FILMING AT INVERARAY

Gareth Neame sees the move to Scotland as a crucial part of keeping the show fresh for the audience. 'When I was traipsing around in Scotland I said to the location manager, "When we designed this show, it was supposed to be shot entirely at Highclere and Ealing. Now I'm wading through a bog in Scotland. How did that happen?" But we have to keep making new stories and doing fresh things with our characters.'

A FAMILY AFFAIR

Scotland offered the audience a chance to see the Crawleys away from Downton and to meet distant relative 'Shrimpy' MacClare, Marquess of Flintshire. Played by Peter Egan (pictured), he is an unhappy aristocrat falling victim to the failing fortunes of his class, but this trip is really an introduction to his wild daughter, Rose, who leaves her family to stay with her relatives at the Abbey.

'Formal dining scenes are always laborious. When you have ten people speaking in one scene, in one room, it naturally gets very tricky to shoot. Having said that, there's a lot of fun to be had in filming them.'

Hugh Bonneville
ROBERT, EARL OF GRANTHAM

The Perfect English Village

Highclere and Ealing both play crucial roles in creating the home of the Crawleys, but also of great importance to the family and their estate workers is the nearby village. The village of Downton is in fact Bampton, which lies rather further from the big house – nearly 30 miles – than is implied on screen. The beauty of Bampton, a picturesque Oxfordshire village, is that the stone of the buildings there is similar in colour to those in Yorkshire, where *Downton* is set.

'It's a very quaint English village,' says 'Sparky' Ellis. 'The reason it works so well is there's the modern part

where all the shops are, but set behind that are some lovely old houses, the village green, the church and the building we use for the exterior of Crawley House.'

Filming for *Downton Abbey* is now such a fixture of village life that cast and crew have made some good friends amongst the locals. So good, in fact, that many actively get involved, according to Ellis. 'The parish council are great and so are the residents. We get the locals into scenes as extras, and the children love seeing us filming.' Several of these villagers enjoyed prime seats in the congregation for Mary and Matthew's wedding.

Downton, like any traditional English village, is orientated around earthly pleasures and the divine: The Dog and Duck pub and the church St Michael and All Angels'. Between those two poles lie the post office and hospital, Crawley House (Isobel's home) and also the Grantham Arms, the pub where Branson memorably refused a bribe from Robert to give up his daughter Sybbie.

While the village is long established, with evidence of its existence dating back to Roman times, Bampton now has a new profile among tourists because of the show.

Coachloads of visitors arrive at the village wanting to wander the same paths as Mary, Violet and the rest. Indeed, walking up Church View you can step into the series' cottage hospital, which you will find is used today as a library, although it was originally built as a village school.

As with any English village, it is the inhabitants, rather than the buildings, that give it life and make it such a pleasure for the cast and crew to film there. 'Bampton's a joy,' says Liz Trubridge. 'The people are so generous-spirited.'

VILLAGE PAST AND PRESENT

On occasion, Mrs Patmore and Daisy are seen running errands in the village; although the majority of food they prepare would have been delivered by local tradesmen, they relish the chance for an excursion. Bampton residents also love venturing into the village during filming, where the atmosphere becomes quite festive.

ALL THE FUN OF THE FAIR

The village green has to be dressed just like any other set, and for the fair scene in series one it was decked out with bunting and lights. In reality, Bampton village is much bigger than it appears on screen, boasting not one, but two churches, a primary school and an art gallery – a rather more sophisticated venue than anything Downton offers.

IT'S ALL IN THE DETAIL

Every care is taken to recreate accurately the period on screen at every location. Look closely and you will see that the outside of Downton's post office is decorated with the iconic wartime recruitment poster exclaiming Lord Kitchener 'Wants You!' The poster has been modified with some graffiti in the aftermath of the war – 'RIP' to fallen soldiers is scrawled across it.

The Village Church

Births, marriages and deaths – village life is punctuated by Christian rites. Bampton's ancient church, St Mary's, has already had starring roles in the Crawley daughters' weddings as St Michael and All Angels', and will reappear in series four.

History permeates its walls. The building is thought to have been built in 1153, but there has probably been a church on the site since before the Norman Conquest.

Filming in a place of worship means treating it with respect, but Liz Trubridge says the best way to proceed is as you would inside any building. 'Wherever we film, we are very aware that it is somebody else's property, and that is no different at St Mary's. We aren't going to work in anybody's home and use a lot of profanities!'

Approval is sought for any changes to the location, too. Before Mary and Matthew's wedding, the crew met with villagers to explain they would be erecting large fences to hide the bride's dress from the paparazzi who were getting creative with cameras on poles!

'I have my modern heroes of lighting,
such as Roger Deakins, who worked on *Skyfall*.
I like to light in a similar way, to make the
show feel more cinematic.'

Nigel Willoughby
DIRECTOR OF PHOTOGRAPHY

Crawley House

Sometimes two locations must be combined in order to create the perfect look for a home on screen. Scenes set inside the rooms of Crawley House are filmed in a house in Beaconsfield, Buckinghamshire, but the exterior belongs to a property in Bampton. 'Both my houses are the envy of the rest of the cast,' Penelope Wilton (Isobel Crawley) laughs. 'They are beautiful, but also the people who own them are extremely nice.'

The relationships between the location owners and the *Downton* team, which are forged by their frequent return to these locations, make for a different experience to those that the cast and crew have had on other shows. John Prendergast explains: 'Often when you finish working at a location you leave and say, "See you later, all done here, thanks very much, ta-ra." Whereas with this show, every location we go to we almost definitely know we will return to it at some point or another. You get to have a good relationship with the owners.'

Endings and Beginnings

Of all the cast, Michelle Dockery has a particular tie to the Bluebell Railway, the heritage steam line in Sussex used to film many station farewells. 'It's a really special place for me because it's where Mary sees Matthew off to war, it's where she has the conversation with Sir Richard Carlisle in series two when he proposes, and she says, "I'll think about it" and then later she goes into labour as she gets off the train. So the railway is very significant and I love filming there.'

Gareth Neame refers to Mary's station goodbye to Matthew, when she gives him her lucky mascot, as 'the most important scene we have made on the show'.

Julian Fellowes agrees. 'I like to write scenes where what the characters are saying is not really what the scene is about,' he explains. 'She was still in love with him and he was probably still in love with her. However, it was also about the fact that he might very well be going off to his death and this might be the last time they saw each other – but none of that was spoken.'

Living it up in London

While the rolling English countryside has its charms, London exerts an increasing pull over the younger Crawleys, who are tempted by the freedom it offers.

For Charles Edwards, who joined the cast in series three as Edith's editor Michael Gregson, their scenes shot in big-city locations have helped to underline how their unconventional relationship is out of place in the rule-bound confines of the Abbey. 'It feels like an affair,' he admits.

In series four the pair visit the Criterion restaurant in Piccadilly – which 'plays' itself – albeit decades earlier. While the Criterion remains a working restaurant today, complete with fabulous interiors, it still had to be dressed as a set, not least because it was packed with its own modern chairs and tables, leaving no room for the film crew's equipment. 'There was a lot of clearing out to do and bringing in of the typical 1920s big palms and fresh flower arrangements,' says Gina Cromwell, the set decorator. 'Then all the tables had to be dressed – using bishop's hat napkins [a traditional way of folding table napkins] and suchlike – to give them the right period feel and look.'

It was a quick turnaround, she remembers, as is often the case in a packed filming schedule. 'The film unit was working in another London location at the time, and we only had one morning to get this scene. We started at about 5 a.m., so it was hard work. We have a lot of those early starts, especially when we are in London.'

'When I first joined the show my scenes were only with Laura Carmichael. We have a little, separate London-based storyline and in a way it doesn't feel much like *Downton*. It feels like an affair, which is what it is.'

Charles Edwards
MICHAEL GREGSON

City Chic

Inside his London flat, Michael Gregson can relax in what is more like a studio space than a conventional sitting room.

Filmed on location in London's Notting Hill and on a set at Ealing, the pale walls and modern sculpture reinforce the distance between his world and Downton's more traditional surroundings.

'That was a fantastic set to dress,' says Gina Cromwell. 'It was really interesting because he wasn't one of the Crawleys, he was a character who had come into the show. We don't quite know what his background is, but he appears to be an intellectually active and educated man. He's obviously wealthy, probably self-made, and has a great, eclectic interest in many things.'

In marked contrast to the Crawleys' heirloom oils and miniatures, Gregson has stocked his own walls. His large grey geometric painting was created by the art department. Cromwell explains that it was inspired by modernist work of the time, from the Vorticism movement.

Using London's Legacies

As with the Criterion, there is little point recreating a set when the real thing is stunningly beautiful – and available for filming.

The iconic façade of St Pancras station in London appears in series four. Part of the relevant sequence – showing Edith disembarking from a period train – was actually shot at the Bluebell Railway, but seamless editing makes it appear as if the scene took place entirely in the capital.

Filming around this busy London transport hub required careful coordination by the crew – not least having to time their presence for early on a Sunday morning to avoid the crowds.

Laura Carmichael, a veteran of shooting at Highclere, relished the change of scene. 'It's so much fun,' she says. 'It feels like another job. It's so different from filming at Highclere, where there are eight or nine characters in a scene. All of a sudden you're at St Pancras with 200 extras and barriers up, just for a scene with me and Charlie [Edwards, who plays Gregson]. You feel incredibly grand.'

ROMANCE AT THE RAILWAY STATION

For Charles Edwards, the station scenes felt like the continuance of a silver-screen tradition: 'It was exactly the way I wanted it to be – waiting for my lover in a trilby and long coat. It's *Brief Encounter*.'

Laura Carmichael also enjoys this illicit romance. 'It is not an easy relationship,' she says. 'Gregson is not a plain-sailing man, but there's passion there. It's a sexier, more passionate affair than with Strallan.'

PARKING PROBLEMS

Just as with any other set, a London exterior is dressed with period cars, street vendors and supporting artists in accurate costume. Impressive as it looks, shooting in the capital brings challenges for a film crew. 'It can cost up to £5,000 just to park everything,' says John Prendergast. 'That includes the crew cars and all of the trailers we need parked as close as possible to the location.'

The Swinging Club Scene

London isn't the only city that offered music and fun. In series four Lady Rose, in an unlikely trio with Anna and Jimmy, finds a dance hall in nearby York.

Although a less fashionable setting than its London counterparts, such a venue would have been popular with local servants and farmworkers, who would have attended afternoon tea dances in their best off-duty outfits.

In reality, this location is miles away from Yorkshire. Hoxton Hall, a nineteenth-century dance hall located in East London's Hackney, was chosen for its period columns, flooring and fire mantels. The exterior was filmed at historic dockyards in Chatham, Kent.

The high-society version of such a club would have been rather different, as scenes at the Lotus Club, frequented by the Crawleys, show overleaf. The location for that venue was the sumptuous ballroom of the Savile Club, a gentleman's club in London's ritzy Mayfair. Still, Rose is happy to be at either venue; at heart the attractions are the same: music and dancing.

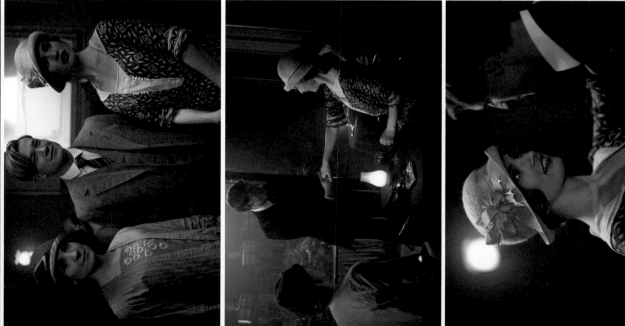

Filming inside London's Savile Club, in its spectacular ballroom, has the advantage of offering a visual freshness to the audience as it will be unfamiliar to most viewers. 'The room is not very recognisable as a location on television, because it doesn't get used for that purpose very much, but it is a beautiful, totally unique space,' says Gareth Neame.

SPLIT LOYALTIES

Shooting at the Savile meant split loyalties for Neame, who is a member of the club. Asked by 'Sparky' Ellis if he could get a discount on the filming fees, the producer had to weigh up his keenness to get a good deal for his show against his desire for his club to get its dues. 'I said, "I'm going to duck out of this. I'm not getting involved either way!"'

'The Savile Club is a beautiful building that's been kept true to its original designs. The club has been at the same location since the 1920s and its elegance remains intact. The members are rightly proud of their building, so to be able to show it off is really pleasing.'

Gareth Neame
EXECUTIVE PRODUCER

Inside
the Prop Store

The Details that Make the Scenes

Downton Abbey demands an enormous number of props to dress the sets and create the feel of the 1920s. But while the Abbey may be modernising – slowly – the props team are not replacing the old with the new.

'With design, there is one school of thought that says that if a show is set in 1922, there should be nothing in the house from before that date. It creates a look like the set of some Bertie Wooster musical, whereas real life isn't like that,' says Julian Fellowes. 'You also have all the things in a house that the family already possess.' So when the props team bring in items to dress the rooms at Highclere, for example, they may add pieces of art or furniture that look as if they were acquired by its residents decades, if not centuries, ago to give a sense of heritage.

A set may demand more contemporary items – for example in Gregson's London flat the art department are conscious that they need to place the location precisely within its time.

By 1925 the term Art Deco had been coined, and by 1928 the building of the iconic Chrysler Building – the pinnacle of that design movement – had begun in New York. But in series four, all this is yet to come. 'With her costumes, Caroline [McCall] is ahead of us in terms of design,' says Donal Woods, the production designer. 'After the war nothing really happened until 1925, when the French exhibition in Paris marked the explosion of Art Deco. Fashion was taking off, but in terms of

> ## 'It's not just about dressing the homes of the rich, but getting good character dressing into the poorer environments, too.'
>
> ### Gina Cromwell
> SET DECORATOR

furniture, design, colours, wallpapers and fabrics it was pretty staid from 1914. We are slowly edging towards a slightly brighter world, but it's a gradual process.'

The key people working for Woods in the props team are the set decorator Gina Cromwell, who is responsible for the detail on set, and the buyer, Sue Morrison, who obtains the necessary items. In terms of sourcing period props, many items are bought, as they are used repeatedly, and kept in the department's vast garage-like store at Ealing. Traditional and antique markets at Kempton Park, Petworth, Dorking and Lincoln, are a useful resource from which they can build up stock.

Online auctions are another source, which are used more and more, albeit with a health warning attached, says Cromwell.

'Personally, I like to see things before I commit to buying them, just because you get a better sense of their size and quality. I have bought things on eBay, but there's a slight risk involved in buying unseen.'

The prop department can also hire items, if necessary. 'We're very lucky in England because we have prophouses, terrific resources that have been built up over years,' says Cromwell. 'They're big warehouses in London largely, and we can hire from them for a short period.'

Many items are created in-house by the art department and the specialist prop makers. Such items can include anything from period product labels, menus and newspapers to everything the Crawleys sit down to eat.

THE REAL-LIFE MRS PATMORE

Lisa Heathcote (on set at Ealing, above) could feed a small army with the amount of food she produces. To ensure continuity through the many takes needed for each scene, she must cook dishes in bulk. For just one dinner in series three, 90 mini-jellies were required, she remembers. 'I made so many because I knew they would melt and not look good after a while.'

COOKING AGAINST THE ELEMENTS

This poultry dish, presented with a Twenties flourish, emerged from Heathcote's kitchen housed inside a truck. She originally used a tent, but the weather was a problem, particularly at Highclere, she says. 'It was a bit like working in a wind tunnel at NASA! One winter, there was actually ice on the gravy. I said, "I think we need to sort this out," so they found me a truck.'

Edible Art

The Crawleys dine in fine style, thanks to food economist Lisa Heathcote, who is responsible for what they eat on screen. 'It's about food and art; I am the hair and make-up person for food,' she laughs.

As delicious as they look, you might not want to eat some of her creations, given her necessary tweaks to them to ensure they last through long hours of filming. A beautiful cake might have a polystyrene base; what looks like whipped cream is likely a sturdier pudding mix, while some dishes are so heavily glazed they are 'solid as a rock!' Here, Twenties food trends come in handy, notes Heathcote. 'They used lots of gelatine and aspic, but I don't make it soft, I make it like concrete. You could technically eat it, but it wouldn't be very nice.'

Heathcote avoids any particularly sugary dishes because they don't last under the hot lights, which was partly why Mary and Edith's ornate wedding cakes were made by specialist modelmakers. Heathcote explains: 'Wedding cakes are fragile things and don't like changes of temperature and being moved a lot, all of which can happen on a film set.'

Vast quantities of food are required to refresh plates for repeated takes. If the Crawleys have lamb chops, says Heathcote, 'I'll probably cook 80, because they'll have to eat them and push them around the plate, and then they start to look a bit sad.' Slicing into huge hunks of meat is avoided, she adds: 'Once you start carving joints, you create problems, because you've got to think about how many times you're going to be doing something.'

Dressing for Dinner

Downton's dinner parties would make the most practised host fret. 'If you are doing a dinner party scene,' Jim Carter (Mr Carson) explains, 'you have to reset the levels of the glasses, the food on the plates, the candles, in every shot for continuity. It's relentless.'

Lisa Heathcote, meanwhile, makes sure the seated actors do not struggle during butler service. 'They're helping themselves, so I have to cut up the food into little, manageable portions,' she says.

These Abbey dinners are usually served on a traditional Spode dinner service, bought by the prop department, and classic manners are observed throughout. 'Food always comes in – and is taken away – from the left, and drink comes in from the right,' notes Alastair Bruce, historical advisor. The menu card is removed after the main course and before the pudding, and the footmen serve with a seat between them, to avoid jostling each other. 'It is old-fashioned, it's the way it's done and we observe it meticulously,' Bruce says.

'I always try to put something inoffensive like watercress or cucumber on the plate so the actors can push it around a bit. Some of them like to tuck in, but they have to remember that once they start eating, they've got to keep doing it each take.'

Lisa Heathcote
FOOD ECONOMIST

MEAGRE OFFERINGS

Cancelled wedding banquets aside, the staff eat very simply. 'Below stairs, they tend to get a lot of bread and cheese, and stew and porridge,' Lisa Heathcote says. 'Apart from when Edith's wedding went wrong and they ate the dishes from the wedding breakfast, there's certainly nothing exciting for them to eat, except leftovers from dinners above stairs.'

CONTINUITY IN THE KITCHEN

What is prepared in kitchen scenes always corresponds to what appears on the table upstairs, notes Heathcote. 'Often I can do a dish that we see in the kitchens, and we see it seconds later above stairs, but the reality is we don't actually film it until three or four weeks later, so I've got to recreate the same dishes again, and make sure they look exactly the same.'

Dishes of the Decade

Mrs Patmore would have produced a 'lot of classic French cuisine', says Heathcote, who draws on period cookbooks for inspiration for the menus, such as *Mrs Beeton's Book of Household Management*.

The house would also have had its own cookbook and would have used recipes that had been passed down over the generations. 'The family would have eaten very well, because they would have been able to get ingredients from the dairy and the home farm, and they would have had wonderful walled gardens filled with vegetables – as well as servants trained to cook them.'

Food is presented just as it would have been in the period, so poultry arrives at the table with its feet still on, while a simple pudding of fruit, biscuits and cream looks like an edible masterpiece. 'They had a finickety way of presenting things to show off their culinary skills – and it's fun,' says Heathcote. 'It's like painting with food.' She may also tweak recipes to make sure they are 'visually strong', such as using mango pieces and berries to brighten up a beige spongy pudding.

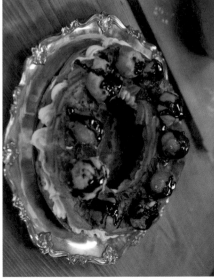

DUBIOUS DISHES
The tables are laid with food destined for the Earl's table, but the cast admit to nibbling on the dishes and ingredients that pass through the kitchen. 'You always regret it!' says Sophie McShera (Daisy). 'You start to think, "How many people have touched that?"'

'What's great is that someone on the props team used to be a chef, so before any kitchen scenes we'll have a chat and he'll show us the techniques he would use when preparing food.'

Matt Milne
ALFRED NUGENT

'Mrs Patmore loathes the mixer, which scares her, but Daisy doesn't – she makes lots of soufflés with it. Daisy is happily embracing all the modern technology.'

Sophie McShera
DAISY MASON

Keeping Up with the Times

The appearance of new props on set helps to reflect the passage of time on screen and can also create quite a stir inside the Abbey. As well as its telephone, Downton now boasts a food mixer, while upstairs the younger generation can listen to music on the gramophone.

Many of these items are actually original pieces that have been carefully restored to look as if they are new. The controversial kitchen mixer was an eBay find, sourced from America, then sent to specialist prop makers who cleaned, stripped and resprayed it. It also had to be rewired by an electrician, both to make it safe and to make it work.

Another piece of Twenties modernity, the gramo-phone (which reappears in series four) was hired. 'It is the gramophone that Mary and Matthew danced to at the end of series two, so I had to make sure that we could get exactly the same one,' says Gina Cromwell.

Not everyone likes this brave new world – and with good reason, says Lesley Nicol, who plays Mrs Patmore, as these kitchen aids reduce the need for staff. 'The introduction of electronic devices scares her because she doesn't know where it will end. None of them know how much their lives will change because of this new technology – and time will later confirm her fears.'

All these new-fangled gadgets were made viable by the more widespread use of electricity, which so alarmed Violet with the threat of 'vapours'. But close inspection of the Ealing set, which recreates her peaceful green drawing room, reveals a period table lamp with a telltale wire. Even the Dowager has begun to accept progress.

Giving Props the Personal Touch

The props team have a keen sense of what suits the taste and environment of each character. Unlike the average buyer of antiques, they have a precise idea of what they need, looking for items that specifically suit locations and characters' individual personalities. 'You can be in a place that's jam-packed with antiques of all sorts – different periods, different uses – and you only see what you want,' says Gina Cromwell. 'It sort of jumps out at you, it's quite amazing. You think, "That's right for such-and-such," so you zone in on it straightaway.'

In particular the team return to dress the sets that return every year, such as Cora and Mary's bedrooms, which have unique looks. Cora's room, as well as being larger than her eldest daughter's, has a more sumptuous, mature feel. The walls feature landscape paintings in

oils and miniatures of ladies in powdered wigs, rather than the flowery decorations that Mary favours.

The calm green interior of Violet's Dower House, meanwhile, harks back to the enthusiasm of an earlier generation for an Eastern-inspired look: 'It's slightly oriental, eighteenth century,' says Cromwell. One purchase in particular had the Dowager's name all over it. 'There's a really beautiful little papier-mâché sewing table that we bought at an antiques market, which is in Violet's house,' she says. 'It's a lovely little thing – Japanese influence, probably eighteenth century. It wasn't a fortune, but as soon as I saw it, I said, "That's it, we have to have that." It's great for her personality.' After all, Violet can be a bit eighteenth century herself, at times.

Motoring à la Mode

Downton's cars are vintage originals, worth hundreds of thousands of pounds. 'The first thing to consider is the script,' says Charmian Adams, the art director. 'Someone drives up in a car: who are they? Do they have a chauffeur? Or are they driving themselves?'

The vehicles, mostly sourced through the specialist company Motorhouse, have also charted the passing of a decade on screen. 'When it came to a new car for the Abbey after the First World War, we went for a new shape – and that limited what was available, because hardly any cars were made during the war. We ended up with a maroon and black Sunbeam.'

Colour is important, with anything garish refused. The cars used to dress Bampton for filming tend to be 'indeterminate' black Ford Model Ts that can appear several times. They also have to be in good working order. When looking at tractors for the fourth series, Adams found one that was perfect but 'when it is hot, it doesn't start.' A no for the Abbey – and for the set, too.

TENDER LOVING REPAIR

The cars' owners, die-hard collectors and enthusiasts, are generally present on set – which means, handily, that there is someone around who can fix them. 'Some of the cars have been continuously maintained over the years, but some were bought as absolute wrecks and their owners have meticulously put them back in order', says Charmian Adams.

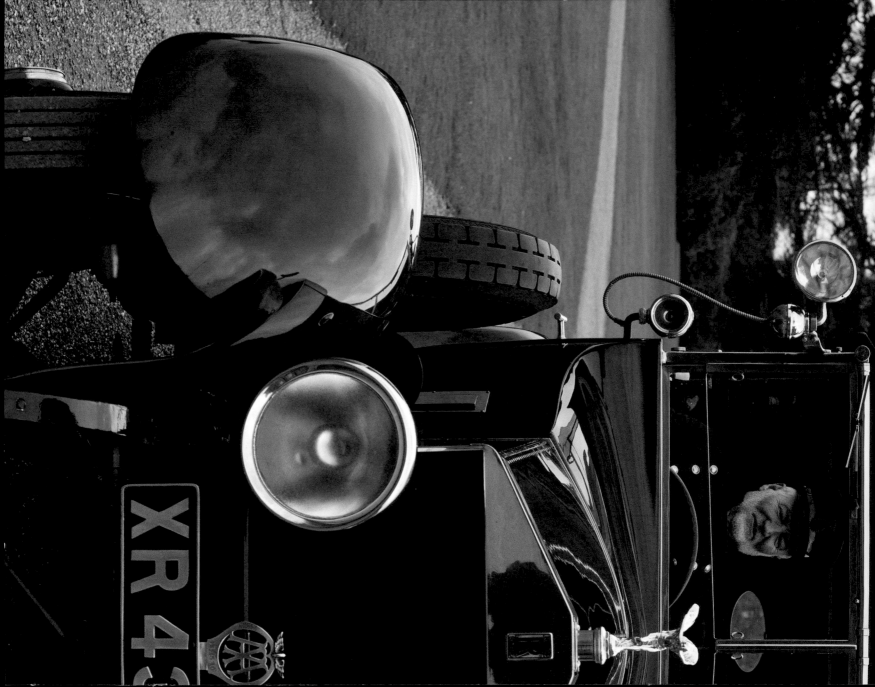

'The cars are originals, taken care of by their owners who are put in costume. If it's not a chauffeur driving, it will be one of the owners. I can't drive, and once, when I had to drive and talk at the same time, I thought I was going to kill a cameraman! I swore terribly.'

Laura Carmichael
LADY EDITH

SOUPING UP THE SOUND

The cars seen on the show may be antiques today, but they were at the cutting edge of engineering in the early twentieth century. So during the post-production process much healthier engine sounds are added to the scenes to give the impression of purring motors. It wouldn't do for Lord Grantham to be ferried about by a sputtering engine, after all.

LONDON LIFE COMES TO DOWNTON

As motor cars became more commonplace, escaping London for the country on a weekend was much more feasible. In series four, Gregson makes a trip to Downton along with newcomers to the show the Duchess of Yeovil (Joanna David), Sampson (Patrick Kennedy), Sir John Bullock (Andrew Alexander) and Anthony Gillingham (Tom Cullen), all pictured above.

Paper, Paper Everywhere

From love letters to newspapers, restaurant menus to patients' records and even the nameplates on the doors to the servants' rooms, *Downton* requires a vast number of print and paper props.

Even if objects are not integral to the plot, they are often made specifically for the show. The newspapers read on screen have been recreated from scans of antique publications kept at the British Library's archive in London, as the originals are too fragile to use on set. 'Can you imagine if someone put their teacup on them?' says Charmian Adams.

The art department may also insert articles into newspapers that are demanded by the script, such as news stories or announcements. Multiple copies of these modified papers are printed by specialist company Data Reprographics.

However, many items are painstakingly handmade at Ealing by Chantelle Valentine, the assistant art director. If, for instance, Robert is reading a letter, it will be one of half a dozen handwritten by her.

Realistic Reproductions

To dress scenes set and shot at London's historic Criterion restaurant, a period menu was sourced from The Ritz hotel replicating what was in vogue at the time. It is very French, as was fashionable, with dishes divided into '*poisons*' and '*legumes*' – although a curry section also offers diners 'Mutton Bombay'.

The art department make free use of historical archives to produce such items, basing another menu on one held in the graphics collection at the Ashmolean Museum in Oxford. The original is not copied exactly; the spacing and the style may be tweaked, or lettering added to suit.

Other such recreations can also be spotted in the Abbey. To stock the boot room, tins of polish came from a hire company, but labels for various bottles were made in-house. 'By the time they are 100 years old, they're pretty tired,' says Charmian Adams. To create fresher-looking packaging, an original label may be scanned and duplicated, but they also design their own packaging from scratch.

Diner à la Carte

HUITRES.

Dressed Crab :: :: 2/-
Saumon fumé :: :: 2/-
Melon de Chypres :: 2/6
Huîtres Américaine :: 5/-
Huîtres Baltimore :: 3/6

Natives (doz.) 5/6
Huîtres Musgrave :: (doz.)

POTAGES.

Fumet de Céleris :: :: 2/-
Potage Bonne Femme (½ doz.) 2/-
Germiny aux Croûtons (doz.) 2/6
Tortue Verte :: :: 3/6

POISSONS.

Délice de Sole Marion :: 3/-
Merlan sur le plat Bercy :: (2 pieces) 5/-
Filet de Maquereau Vénitienne :: 2/6
Médaillon de Turbotin au Sherry :: 3/-
Truite au Bleu :: 5/-
Sole Normande :: (2 persons) 10/-

ENTRÉES.

Turbot poché, Sce. Divine :: 3/6
Truite de Rivière aux Auberg :: 3/-
Suprême de Barbue Florentine :: 3/6
Raiton au Beurre d'Isigny :: 3/-
Homard Thermidor :: 4/-
Eperlans Polonaise :: 7/-
:: :: 12/-
:: :: 30/-

Tête de Veau Archiduc :: ::
sautés de Ris d'Agneau Bérrichonne ::
de Ris de Veau ::
Langue de Veau ::
Bordeaux au Porto ::
Crème aux Petits Pois Paysanne :: 15/-
France Dorothy ::

CURRIES.

Poulet de Grain Chevalière ::
Tête de Veau Poulette ::
Jambon d'york au Clicquot ::
Tournedos sautés Pré-Catelan ::
Salmis de Gibier Garde Chasse ::
Suprême de Volaille Staël ::
Perdreau Cocotte Bonne-Maman :: 8/-
Rable de Lièvre Polonaise :: 3/-

Mutton Bombay :: ::
Prawns Calcutta :: ::

ROTIS.

Reine :: :: 21/-
Pigeon de Bordeaux :: 7/-
Rable de Lièvre :: 7/-

LEGUMES.

Céleris braisés :: :: 2/6
Carottes à la Crême :: 2/6
Laitues au Jus :: 2/6
Courgettes Hollandaise :: 2/6
Aubergine frite :: 3/-

Grouse sur Canapé
Aylesbury Canapé
Perdreau Feuilles de Vign

ENTREMETS

:: :: 4/-
:: :: 3/-
:: 3/6

Jambon de Bayonne :: 2/-
Hors d'Œuvre Variés :: 3/-
Grape Fruit Savoy :: 2/6
Caviar frais :: 2/6

Consommé Bohémienne ::
Croûte au Pot Parisienne ::
Ox-Tail au Sherry ::
La Marmite ::

Pommes Lon
Pommes
Pommes

Lady Mary Crawley,
Downton Abbey,
Downton,
Yorkshire.

Mrs. Reginald Crawley,
Crawley House,
Downton.

The Dowager
Downton
Yorkshire

Proper Post

A letter may just be glimpsed on screen, but its contents always correspond to the action. Michelle Dockery (Mary) says: 'When we're reading or writing a letter, you can really get into character through the detail in the props.'

So if someone has just received an invitation to tea, that will be communicated in writing, in an appropriate hand. 'It's very beautiful, delicate script for the girls, while the men tend to have a more hurried style – though Matthew's was looser and more dreamy,' says Chantelle Valentine. Valentine makes hundreds of envelopes, as those used at the time would have been much smaller than those used today. Filming requires multiple copies of the same letter, sometimes up to 15, so the actor can open up a fresh one for each take.

Alastair Bruce, meanwhile, ensures that the forms of address are correct. A letter to Violet, for instance, should be sent to: 'The Dowager Countess of Grantham, The Dower House, Downton, Yorkshire', with no postcode.

Inside
the Wardrobe

Something Old, Something New

Downton's wardrobe room at Ealing Studios is a hive of activity overseen by Caroline McCall, the show's Emmy Award-winning costume designer (pictured opposite with Maggie Smith).

Gareth Neame sees her work as a vital element of the show's success: 'The costume designer is really part of the producing team, because she has a huge amount to do with the telling of the story.'

While many items are found at vintage fairs or are hired from costume houses, much is created for the show. McCall explains: 'It's incredibly difficult to find enough clothes from this period; the fabrics are so delicate that they've perished. Also, because this look was fashionable in the Seventies, they are just not around any more.'

When a period piece is tracked down, it is unlikely to be ready to wear. 'Usually they need a lot of love, or are turned into another garment. For the female principals, the majority of clothes in the fourth series have been sourced and manipulated to make other items, or have been made from scratch.'

THE PERFECT FIT

The costume department are busy for months before filming begins, creating outfits and holding fittings for all the cast members. 'We know their sizes, but we need to check proportions – Cora, for example, tends to keep the neckline higher,' says Sarah Humphrey, who as the cutter is kept busy sewing items. 'Normally we fit the actors a day or two before they wear their clothes.'

HISTORY IN THE DETAIL

Although many dresses are created especially for the show, they often incorporate pieces of fabric that are decades old. Inspiration comes from myriad contemporary sources, from detailed illustrations to black-and-white stills. 'There are certain images that reappear and reappear,' says Heather Leat, the costume supervisor. 'You are looking for something new, something you haven't seen before.'

Getting into Character

Downton's historically accurate costumes establish a sense of period but they also play a crucial part in helping the cast get into character. 'It's an incredible thing to wear an evening dress and immediately feel you are back in that time,' says Lily James (Rose). 'The cut, the feel of it changes the way you move.'

Even if every detail may not be obvious to the viewer, the care that goes into personalising a character's wardrobe is invaluable to the actors. 'I really loved an outfit I wore in the episode at the end of series three,' says James. 'I had a metallic, gold-bronze flowery evening dress and a crown-like piece on my head to match. Caroline [McCall] often gives me rose earrings, rose necklaces, and that dress in particular was in a gold metallic fabric with purple roses embroidered on it.'

As well as reflecting her namesake flower, the wardrobe created for Downton's youngest family member also hints at her love of all things modern. 'Rose wears a lot of knitwear in series four; apparently everyone was going wild for it in the Twenties,' notes James. Not everyone is as much of a fan as her character, however, with Maggie Smith commenting that one outfit looked 'like a kettle, a tea cosy, or something'.

For Michelle Dockery (Mary), the clothes really set the scene. 'They're beautiful dresses. I think Caroline has surpassed herself, again. In series four there is an embracing of the Twenties; there's a real change. There is a sense of the war being over and everyone being in celebration – but obviously not Mary, yet.'

'Rose is a bit of a rebel, pushing at the boundaries. She's not making her point through politics, but through dancing and drinking. She wants to be free and have fun.'

Lily James
LADY ROSE

COSTUME DESIGN

Creating the Look

Carefully curated inspiration boards of images and fabric swatches lie behind each character's style.

'I've got loads of magazines from the period, lots of photographs, and piles of research,' says Caroline McCall. 'When you start to put boards together you think, "Oh, that looks like Cora," or, "That looks like Isobel," and you get ideas together. As the series goes on, it's quite funny, looking at my boards and saying, "Oh, we've done that for Mary, we've made that for Cora."'

McCall also has to consider how the individual looks will work in an ensemble. 'I try to keep people to a palette and then it makes it easier to put everybody together in a room – but sometimes it doesn't work that way,' says McCall.

'For eveningwear in series four, Mary is in black or grey or purple, when normally I would put her in blues and deep pinks. So Cora has been in blues and dark pinks. Edith I tend to put in corals and greens, Rose is blues and pinks as well, while Violet wears a lot of purple and greeny blues.'

'I see how Caroline McCall dresses these ladies and I think they look fantastic. She has a great eye and knows what suits each actress's shape, style and colouring.'

Gareth Neame
EXECUTIVE PRODUCER

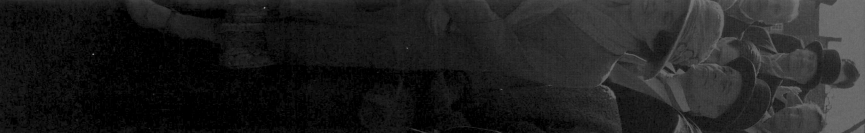

'Those' Dresses

'I knew they'd have to be quite different,' McCall says of the sisters' bridal looks. 'The big fashion for wedding dresses at the time was lace or satin. I knew that lace would particularly suit Mary, and I thought that satin would be better for Edith. So that's how the designs for the dresses began.'

Conscious that Mary would be seen walking down the grand staircase, McCall wanted her 'to shimmer and sparkle' in the light from the window. 'Previously we'd used lace with a silver thread through it and I thought that would work really well.'

For Edith, the dress was designed around an original train covered with flowers and crystals, with these motifs repeated on the gown. The idea, says McCall, was that her older groom, Sir Anthony Strallan, would think, 'Oh my goodness, how beautiful,' before he jilted her. 'It's not "I can't marry you," it's "I can't marry you, because look how beautiful and young you are, and how much life you have ahead of you" – although none of that is said.'

A TALE OF TWO BRIDES

McCall wanted to use Mary's wardrobe to give her a new identity as she enters into married life. 'Mary had been hard and quite cold, but I didn't want to see any of that in her wedding dress. I wanted it to be soft, understated, delicate and romantic.' Edith, on the other hand, not only had to look like a beautiful bride but some thought had to go into how the episode unfolded. So Edith's dress was designed so that even when, devastated, she sobs on a bed after the abortive church ceremony, 'it looks really beautiful and gorgeous!'

'The detail on the dress was extraordinary. It was incredibly fragile, and because of all the work that had gone into it we were really careful. It was very much how you would treat your own wedding dress.'

Michelle Dockery
LADY MARY

Bright Young Things

After the end of the First World War, myriad possibilities and freedoms begin to open up for the younger members of the house, and much of this new lifestyle was to be found in London. 'Downton very much represents the "country", a kind of stereotypical aristocracy, but in London the Bloomsbury Set are gathering – the writers, the artists and musicians – there is a new freedom of expression on offer,' explains Caroline McCall.

Fashions in the capital reflect the explosion of creativity taking place as the old social boundaries start to crumble. 'With this new modernism came self-expression through clothes – there were lots of prints and bright colours,' says McCall. 'We've tried to convey, through both Edith's and Rose's wardrobe, this new wave that's coming in.'

Laura Carmichael feels 'incredibly lucky' in her wardrobe as her character spends more time in the capital. 'She's shopping in London to look nice for her lover, and it's such an exciting period of change for clothes that Caroline's been keen to show,' she says. 'In London Edith would have been seeing the fashionable set – the bohemians, Virginia Woolf and the rest – who were on the cutting edge of what was socially accept-able. It's far more risqué and a lot freer.'

As McCall explains, Edith is living 'a life that those at Downton see as well as her London life'. So Edith is wearing more prints, as well as pieces 'she would never wear at Downton, because they're quite shocking'. She may not be quite the rebel Sybil was – but she is follow-ing her lead in becoming a woman of the times.

Branson – Moving Up the Ranks

Nothing illustrates Tom Branson's social ascent from the Crawleys' chauffeur to their son-in-law so clearly as his changing wardrobe.

In the early 1920s, clothes were an important indicator of a person's social status. 'The cast found it hilarious that one of the storylines in series four was about gloves,' Alastair Bruce relates. 'But these details were terribly important in those days – they reflected status and where you stood in the social order.'

Tom's new wardrobe shows the world that he is prepared to assimilate into Sybil's family – however politically conflicted he feels – but it also highlights the fact that he is not born to the role of country gentleman. 'We show this in the choice of fabrics for Tom – they're not quite aristocracy,' explains Caroline McCall. 'He's got this brown knickerbocker suit that he wears, while if he was an aristocrat he'd be in green tweed. The fabric is more Irish working class. That's a conscious decision that Allen [Leech, who plays Tom] and I made together.'

'A lot of what we do is driven by costume, so Caroline McCall and I talk upfront and work out a basic colour palette. Once I know what that is, I'll work to make each scene complement it.'

Nigel Willoughby
DIRECTOR OF PHOTOGRAPHY

The Fashion of Mourning

'Simplicity is key to Mary's style,' says McCall. 'Classic yet fashionable.' But this look shifts from simple to stark in the wake of Matthew's death, as her wardrobe reflects her newly widowed status. As the fourth series opens, Mary is in full mourning dress – all black – which after a period of time lifts into the shades of half-mourning, 'purples and mauves, and greys and black and white – quite monochrome', says McCall.

Isobel Crawley, of course, is also devastated by the loss of Matthew, and again her wardrobe reflects her grief at her son's death. 'We've kept the same silhouette as in the last series, but have used different fabrics and now her whole wardrobe is black,' says McCall.

The speed at which people moved through the stages of mourning would have had an impact on how they were perceived by the wider world, a point that the show's storylines acknowledge.

As Julian Fellowes notes, 'The relentless mourning of the Victorians was going out of fashion, but this custom of going from mourning into half-mourning, then into normal dress survived until the second war. A cousin of my grandfather's, whom I knew very well, never came out of half-mourning. It was a mark of affection to her late husband. She felt that dressing in half-mourning was less of an aggressive statement than being in deepest black.' Still, he notes, his great-grandmother, widowed at 39 by a carriage accident, 'stayed in black for the rest of her life. Being in black wasn't unusual, whereas it's always taught that it was absolutely extraordinary.'

'Mary's style is often very simple and elegant. Because of everything that has happened to her she has become less vain with each series.'

Michelle Dockery
LADY MARY

Updating the Uniforms

In contrast to the more varied palette upstairs, the below-stairs women's uniforms range from black for the housekeeping staff to earthy tones for the kitchen workers.

Nonetheless, their costumes subtly reflect the changing period as the series goes on, with their hemlines inching up.

'I must have had about two or three costume fittings,' says Phyllis Logan of series four. 'We did wear original dresses at first, but they began to come apart from constant use. So now the costume department have made our uniforms using patterns created from original outfits.'

Despite the changing times, there is little chance of the senior female staff giving up their corsets – 'sadly!' says Lesley Nicol. 'The thing is that a woman of that age, including Mrs Hughes, would find it difficult to lose their corset. At the moment, we are sticking with them, but it is nice to take them off at the end of filming.' She is fonder of Mrs Patmore's kitchen cap: 'I love that hat. It reminds me of Andy Pandy.'

Dressing to Impress

If modern-day visitors were to arrive at Twenties' Downton Abbey, they might struggle to tell exactly who belonged above stairs and who was from below, given the stylish appearance of some staff.

The footmen in particular are dressed to impress, because their duties put them on show to the family and their guests. 'You are the peacocks of the house and the front of the house. At all times you must appear immaculate. The moment you put on those tails, the penguin suit and the stiff collar, you start to find yourself,' says Ed Speleers (Jimmy).

The staff can be even bigger sticklers for formality than their employers, of course, with Mr Carson always dressing for dinner even though he will be serving it. As the butler, he is particularly resistant to change. 'Of everybody, I don't think my appearance has changed in four series,' says Jim Carter. 'It's exactly the same costume. The day shirt is a bit softer than the evening shirt, which is starched like cast iron. It makes your bearing more upright.'

Off Duty and Out of the Abbey

The below-stairs cast joke of 'costume envy', citing the glorious creations worn by the ladies at the Abbey. After all, even when they are out of their work clothes, their characters do not have the time or means to follow fashion like their employers. 'They don't get out that often,' laughs Caroline McCall.

The scripts rarely offer situations in which the servants can enjoy the fun side of life, but when they do, the actors relish the opportunity to dress up – just as their servant characters would have done. 'For the servants' ball we each got a dress to wear,' says Lesley Nicol. 'It was hilarious, rather like having an office party with everyone saying, "Oh, you look nice!"'

Ed Speleers says his character Jimmy seeks out 'any opportunity to take the edge off', which includes getting out of his stiffly starched work shirts. 'He goes out a fair bit, and he's got a nice three-piece suit.' When Jimmy is out of uniform, his body language becomes looser, says Speleers: 'One of this shoulders might drop a bit and he appears more relaxed.'

Marvellous Millinery

You are never fully dressed without a hat – at least, not at Downton Abbey, where to wander around bareheaded outside the grounds would have invited comment. Whether they are off to church or on a social visit, the Crawley ladies just do not leave the house half-dressed. Even their servants put on a hat for the briefest trip into the village.

People at that time would not have thought twice about it, explains Alastair Bruce, the historical advisor, citing a scene filmed for series four in which two characters head for the door after a shocking incident. 'And I said, "But where are their coats and hats?" So we had to get that in and create that action. When you leave a house like that you put on your coat and hat.'

'The lady's maid would put the hat on her mistress, then the lady would go out to see her friends and she would not take it off until she returned home.'

Alastair Bruce
HISTORICAL ADVISOR

Luckily, this period offers the costume department a multitude of millinery choices.

Nothing beats that icon of Twenties fashion, the cloche. The small, neat, face-framing hat, named for the French for 'bell', proved enduringly popular. 'Cloche hats were really fashionable in the early Twenties,' says McCall. 'You wouldn't have seen the really tiny hats, they came later in the decade. And the wide-brimmed, romantic hats were still around.'

These bigger, sweeping hats do not represent a more traditional look, she says, so much as reflect the variety of looks in circulation following the turbulent war years. In general terms, the look for women in this era is getting sleeker about the head, in contrast, say,

to the really wide, flower-brimmed hats that Cora used to wear to top the longer, more fitted dresses of earlier years. Magi Vaughan, make-up and hair designer, explains that for practical reasons the cloche influenced the new sleeker hairstyles: 'If you are wearing a cloche you can't have a high bun. The hair has to be really low and tight to the neck, otherwise the hat will never go on.'

Which hat best suits each character is taken into consideration, too. Violet, for instance, wears her hats set forward on the head and at an angle, and they are often more formal creations than those of her granddaughters. You will not see the Dowager leaving the house in a cloche, while equally Mary, who favours simplicity in her outfits, would never wear anything festooned with fake grapes. It comes as no surprise that the most outlandish hats seen so far have been showcased by Cora's mother, Martha.

The style of a hat mattered, for once it was pinned firmly in place on the head with around 15 pins, it would stay on until the lady returned home. 'The lady's maid would put the hat on her mistress, then the lady would go out to see her friends and she would not take it off until she returned home,' says Bruce. 'If people came to lunch at Downton they would have their hats on, while those who lived at Downton would not.'

As for men, they almost always wear hats out of doors, says Bruce. 'They would remove them if they met a woman, and would take off their hat and gloves if they went into a house.' Here again, social status plays a role. Robert's white tie would be finished with a top hat, something Mr Carson would never wear. 'In full dress, a gentleman wore a top hat, whereas a butler would have worn a bowler hat,' notes Bruce. 'It would be presumptuous for a butler to wear a top hat.'

WEDDING HATS

Mary was not the only one looking soft and romantic at her wedding. Making up the bridal party, her mother and sisters wore loose dresses in a delicate, muted palette, their outfits finished with wide-brimmed hats covered in ruching and cloth flowers.

CLOCHE-STYLE HATS

Felt cloche hats offered a more everyday option for ladies, but even so they were not devoid of ornament, with the neat shapes set off by wide ribbons and jaunty feathers.

Dressing for Dinner

Empires rise and fall, wars are won and lost – but the Crawleys still change for dinner. Elizabeth McGovern is a particular fan of the dresses that she gets to wear as Cora. 'They are still very up-and-down straight, boyish and flat-chested with no waist whatsoever,' she says. 'There is a lot of really exquisite beading and beautiful colours and fabrics.'

There is a lot of them.

A total of 44 evening dresses were needed for just two episodes of series four alone. The above-stairs ladies also boast up to six pairs of shoes each, while those below stairs are lucky to own one or two pairs.

'The creation of the dresses' intricate beading is outsourced to a specialist, but much of the other costume work is done by the cutter, Sarah Humphrey. She concentrates on creating wardrobes for Mary and Isobel. In this new decade, the dresses remain elegant and detailed, but they are also becoming more modern. As Laura Carmichael notes, 'Some of them feel daring even today. They are quite low-cut!'

Introducing 'Beadith'

Seeming to hang from just a string of pearly beads, the dress Edith wears to a London restaurant in series four was affectionately nicknamed 'Beadith' by the costume department.

Its roots lay in a piece of fabric and a period illustration, and its story underlines the organic way in which the show's looks are created. 'We wanted to see Edith in something completely different and really quite racy,' explains McCall. 'I'd found a beaded and sequined piece of fabric in Paris and bought it; it was falling apart and had to be remounted. Then I was looking at illustrations from the time by French artist George Barbier, which show a lot of flesh being exposed, and that's what I wanted to do.'

That piece of beading was sewn into a bodice, then the rest of the dress was built around it using chiffon. Charles Edwards (Gregson) commented that during filming Edith's dresses needed 'a lot of care and attention – Caroline McCall was always there in between takes, sewing a stitch'.

Dedicated Followers of Fashion

They may be tucked away in the Yorkshire countryside, but that is no obstacle to the Abbey's ladies being able to follow the latest fashions.

Like the rest of the English aristocracy, the Crawley women would have been aware of current trends driven by the big-name Paris-based designers, who included Vionnet, Lanvin and Beer – Coco Chanel was yet to reach the height of her popularity. 'There were lots of designers around with quite different styles – it was a really interesting period in fashion,' Caroline McCall reveals.

Dubbed the queen of draping, Madeleine Vionnet invented the bias cut, while fellow Frenchwoman Jeanne Lanvin was known for her fabulous embellishments and muted palette. The house of Beer was founded by a German designer, Gustav Beer, but was based in Paris.

A trip to Paris to expand their wardrobes would not have been out of the question for the Crawleys, says McCall. 'They could have gone to see a collection and then had pieces made; they had that kind of money.'

AN OUTFIT FOR EVERY OCCASION
The aristocratic lifestyle afforded plenty of opportunity for competitive dressing, at a cost. The daily activities each demanded a different outfit, whether in the country at Downton Abbey, or in London at Lady Rosamund's home (opposite), requiring a large – and expensive – wardrobe.

'I love the style of the dresses
– it's a great-looking period.
The costumes in series four
have been more beautiful and
inventive than ever.'

Elizabeth McGovern
CORA, COUNTESS OF GRANTHAM

Cora, Countess of Grantham

Having married into the English
aristocracy, Cora is very much
established in her adopted
society – yet she still retains
something of her outsider's
perspective. As an American, she
is more willing to embrace change
than her husband Robert, while
her wealthy background means she
has real spending power.

Her wardrobe reflects all this,
says McCall. 'Cora is very elegant
and sophisticated, yet she's quite
modern in her approach to clothes
– which you see when guests visit.
She's more fashionable than other
people, because she's American
and has money – and she has a
sense of style.' That, after all,
cannot be bought.

'You find you become informed about the era by your costume; it's all there in every little detail'.

Hugh Bonneville

Robert, Earl of Grantham

Just as much care is taken over the men's clothing as the women's. Hugh Bonneville remembers that a waistcoat he wore in series two was the subject of lengthy talks between the costume department and Julian Fellowes, with regards to it being white or cream.

'I would far rather hear that level of discussion and detail than a producer like Julian saying, "Oh actually, no one will notice, make it orange, it doesn't matter," he says. 'This is again one of the reasons why *Downton Abbey* has clicked in the way that it has – there is such an attention to detail. Even though we get things wrong – of course we do – there's an aspiration to be as accurate as possible.'

Inside the Wardrobe Truck

Shuttling between Ealing, High-clere and all the other varied locations, the wardrobe truck is a vital part of the cavalcade, storing the principal characters' main costumes and accessories, as well as those of guest stars.

The packed rails tell the story of *Downton* through clothes, from the military uni-forms once worn by the Abbey's men during the war, to the tiny woollen garments tagged 'baby Sybbie'. Labels on stacked drawers list everything from 'coloured long and short socks' to posher fabrics, 'silk, satin, chiffon', along with the latest change sheets, which set out what is needed to dress each actor in their upcoming scenes.

The truck is kept in order by the wardrobe mistress, Asia Macey, who spends her days setting out costumes,

'All the costumes are incredible. Last year we did a scene in Scotland by the loch; everyone was in tweeds and walking clothes and the women had furs and hats – that was beautiful.'

Asia Macey
WARDROBE MISTRESS

washing and maintaining the clothes and helping to dress the actors. Dressing gowns are kept on hand for the cast as they get in and out of costume, while extra warmth is often needed during filming. 'You can't always be in thick coats for filming, so in cold weather it's a nightmare working outside – we have to wear endless underwear!' says Pe-nelope Wilton (Isobel). 'I was on a station platform for a day and it was perishing. People race around with hot-water bottles to put down your clothes.'

Certainly, the process behind the *Downton* look is not always as glamorous as the end result. 'The corsets are uncomfortable,' admits Macey, 'but many of the actors are now used to them.'

COSTUME CARE

Using original costumes from the period demands particular vigilance when they are worn on set. Macey says, 'They are very fragile and can get damaged, so you have to keep stitching and fixing them to get them through the scenes.'

WARDROBES BURSTING AT THE SEAMS

The racks underline just how many more clothes the family have compared with their staff – there are outfits for daytime, for hunting, and for evening and other formal occasions.

'What are my favourite pieces?
It's not always just the pretty
evening dresses – some of the
jewellery is incredible and also the
array of beautiful, tailored coats.
There's not much original costume
left from the very early Twenties, so
it's a special period to work on.'

Asia Macey
WARDROBE MISTRESS

Perks of the Job

Cloth for a frock was the present Mary handed Anna one Christmas, as was the tradition at many great houses, but that was not the only way by which she added to her maid's wardrobe.

If eagle-eyed viewers think some of Anna's outfits look familiar, that is no coincidence. 'Quite often, employers passed on clothes to their lady's maid or to their staff when they were finished with them,' says McCall. 'At Matthew and Mary's wedding, Anna wore an old dress of Mary's that had been altered for her. Often the garments would be remodelled into something else.'

Most of the time, however, we see Anna in her all-black maid's outfit. For a typical day of filming, her change sheet lists a lace-back corset, a black sleeveless slip, a stiff black silk skirt and matching blouse, T-bar leather shoes and Anna's gold pendant.

For practicality, the costume team may use some modern-day items – if hidden from sight – such as black tights, rather than stockings, and store-bought slips.

Taking on a New Shape

The most visual way by which the series charts the passage of time is of course through fashion.

However, Caroline McCall is also careful to maintain continuity, so she has made sure that the look that she established for the post-war episodes has been carried through to the fourth series. She explains: 'All the characters are maintaining that look, but some of them are starting to take it just a little bit further, to modernise.'

It is a period rich in choices for the costume team. 'It's more difficult in the early Twenties to say, "This is the fashion," because after the war there were so many things going on,' she says. 'You look at the fashion magazines and the different influences, and you can't quite believe the number of styles that were popular at that time. When you get to the mid-Twenties you very definitely get to a point of, "Oh, these dresses are a lot shorter" and you're into the famous flapper dresses. But there's still much more freedom, it would seem, in what people are wearing in the early Twenties.'

DIGNITY AT THE DANCE

Although we are into a new decade, it is not quite the Roaring Twenties – yet. The dresses remain very long, and the shockingly high hemlines famous of this decade – and all that they signified – are some time away. Caroline McCall thinks this is an important time for fashion: 'They are truly beautiful clothes; more so than in the mid- to late-Twenties when it gets really boyish, with the "flapper" style.'

The Rise of Black Tie

Just as women's dress shapes soften at the beginning of this decade, the rules around men's wardrobes are also relaxing, particularly for formal wear. For evening, the obligatory white tie and a tailcoat is slowly ceding ground to the dinner jacket – much to the Dowager's horror.

'Through the Twenties and Thirties white and black tie lived alongside each other, then white tie vanished during the Second World War,' says Julian Fellowes. 'What I rather like is that black tie, when it first appeared, was essentially a less formal option, what we would think of as informal chic. Violet hates black tie because she regards it as a sign that everything is coming apart.'

While we may smile at Violet's resistance to change, she has a point, Fellowes notes. 'One of the reasons she has a point, Fellowes notes. 'One of the reasons the old system came to an end is that a great swathe of the upper class didn't want to play any more, they didn't want to have their lives dominated by when luncheon had to be served and all the rest of it.' Still, it is all very different to what we would consider casual today.

While some of the menswear is hired from Cosprop, a costume house, various tailcoats and waistcoats worn on screen are original pieces. The upstairs cast say this formal wear helps them establish themselves in the period – including how they hold their bodies.

The costume, says Charles Edwards, 'immediately lifts your posture. The starched shirtfront is such that it makes you stand ramrod straight. I tend to slouch, so after a couple of days' filming I get backache just from holding this position. It's very, very helpful in terms of placing you in the world of the character.'

The Timeless Elegance of the Dowager Countess

No one would expect the Dowager Countess to be following the latest trends, but her style does change with the times. 'Violet, who essentially thinks the world is going from bad to worse, wears clothes that are suggestive of the Edwardian era, although in fact they are in a Twenties cut,' Julian Fellowes explains. Caroline McCall agrees: 'Of course, Violet very much stays an Edwardian woman, but her clothes have got softer as the series have gone on and are a little less structured – a hint at the Twenties in terms of the weight of the fabrics.'

While purple is the colour of half-mourning, we see Violet in this shade simply 'because it's a colour she likes', says McCall. 'Violet wears mostly purples, greens and greys, because they are colours that suit her.' Crucial to Violet's silhouette is her silver-handled walking stick. Unlike Mr Bates, whose stick has changed throughout the show, the Dowager is wedded to her more elegant choice. There is no spare, so the props team keep a keen eye on it, assiduously storing it on their 'stand-by' truck every night.

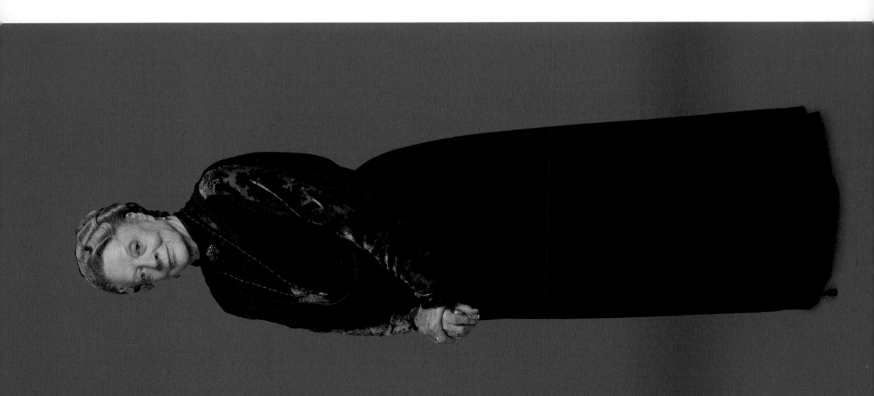

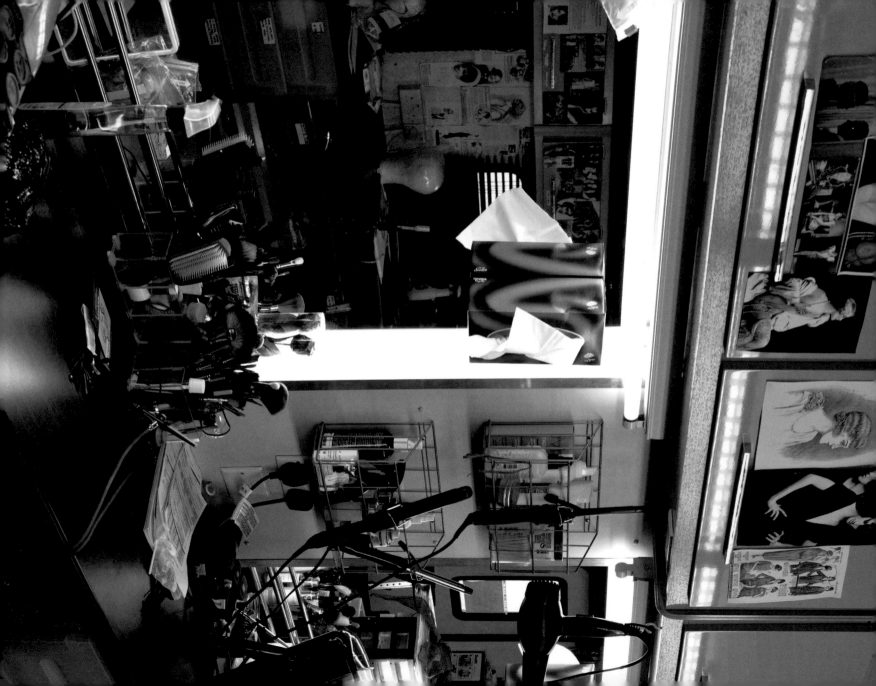

Inside
Hair & Make-up

The Faces of *Downton Abbey*

The female cast members of *Downton Abbey* have a reliance on cosmetics that would have shocked their real-life counterparts in the early twentieth century. In this era, they would not have been privy to the mysteries of cosmetics because it was not deemed to be a part of the respectable lady's toilette.

This provides quite a challenge for the make-up team, as the actors need some lift and colour for the cameras, but they can't appear to be 'made-up'. 'If a lady looked like she was wearing make-up, she could be a prostitute,' explains Magi Vaughan, the show's hair and make-up designer. 'So you don't want to go there!' Therefore the end result is deliberately a subtle, restrained, 'muted' effect, one that Vaughan cre-

> **'It's like creating a painting … we're copying a portrait from the time, in which the face looks perfect, but we are trying not to make it look too stiff.'**
>
> **Magi Vaughan**
> HAIR AND MAKE-UP DESIGNER

ates through the use of shades inspired by images of women on posters of the time.

The key to the *Downton* look, as Vaughan sees it, is the make-up base – a flawless finish that appears that way for a reason: all the make-up artists wield actual airbrushes. 'The whole idea is to keep the skin looking rather perfect but not deliberately made-up,' she says. 'The airbrush make-up is very, very fine, and it just evens everything out. It's like creating a painting.' Powder is a no-no. 'It sort of deadens the face,' says Vaughan. In her quest for a fresher look, particularly on the younger characters, she even draws freckles on Lily James (Rose) to emphasise her youth.

Subtle pink tones help achieve the natural effect, which is executed by Vaughan and a five-strong team. 'I put a lot of glow in the skin so the light just picks it up, which gives you that porcelain look. It's a pale pink that has no shimmer in it. It's as if you were naturally blushing – but in a most beautiful way – and if you look at paintings of that period, you see that gorgeous blush going on. So that's what I'm trying to re-create.'

The Crawley women also wear false eyelashes, each lash individually applied. While the ladies of a great house in that era would not have worn these, of course, they work to 'open their eyes' on screen. It is certainly a more discreet approach than using the soot-based concoctions that were popular at the time as a primitive form of mascara.

As for the maids, the look is even more natural, because at this time the household staff would have

been completely bare-faced. For the female servants the team do little more than airbrush them with a base.

A keen eye is also kept on anything in the actors' appearance that would be out of place and too modern for the period. 'You've got to be very careful with eyebrows,' says Vaughan. 'They must not be too plucked, too shaped or anything like that, which they wouldn't have been at the time. We spend a bit of time getting that right.'

Even as the series swings into the Twenties and leaves the gloomy war and post-war years behind, make-up still remains simple and understated. Natural colours continue to dominate the scheme and the make-up artists will avoid the more dramatic look that many associate with this decade for a while longer. *Downton Abbey* is not yet embroiled in the revelatory era of the flapper – it is a few years away yet.

Staying Picture Perfect

'CHECKS please!' At this cry, Magi Vaughan (opposite) and a small army of make-up artists, with brushes and cosmetics spilling from see-through bags, leap up and rush onto the set. Quickly working around the cast, they remove some shine here, tweak a curl of hair there – all to ensure continuity in scenes that can be shot hours or even weeks apart – before returning to their positions, poised for the next filming break.

On busy filming days the make-up truck can seat six actors for pre-camera prepping, a process that can take an hour or more at the beginning of the day – particularly for the women. But this is just the start of the process, because the actors will also need their 'checks' between takes.

At the end of a long day the actors finally return to the chairs in the truck for 'de-rigging'. This is when the team will carefully unpin any hair pieces, then remove make-up. As a final touch, their faces are cleansed, toned and moisturised before the actors are sent on their way.

Turning the Tide of Fashion: The Marcel Wave

To Magi Vaughan's mind, lady's maid Anna has set the latest fashion at the Abbey. It is she who has dressed the ladies' hair with the Marcel wave, having seen it done in Paris when accompanying Mary and Matthew on honeymoon. Named after the man who created the look, this hairstyle – formal, sculptured waves lying close to the head – is synonymous with the glamour and style of the emerging Twenties. 'I knew that in the storyline they had honeymooned in France,' Vaughan explains. 'Although Mr Marcel – a French hairdresser – had created this look almost 50 years earlier, it had only just become *the* style. I decided, "Oh, Mary and Anna would have seen that" and they would have wanted to replicate it. So it was an excuse to bring the Marcel to Downton, really.'

The look had been created by Monsieur Marcel (various versions of his full name circulated) as a way to artificially re-create the pretty wave of his mother's hair. He used hot irons and discovered that the advantage of his technique over others, such as shaping the hair with wet combs and leaving it to dry undisturbed, was that because it was set by heat the style would last and last.

Over time, the Marcel wave would also become associated with the increasingly popular bob cut, when women who had dared to crop their hair often showed it off in Marcel's rigid waves.

In series four, *Downton* is still in the era of long hair, although the ladies' appearances can be deceptive, as their more traditional up-dos give way to a sleeker look in the years after the war. 'We're not quite at the stage where people started actually bobbing their hair,' says Vaughan. 'They kept their hair long and tried to make

it look like a bob. But they wouldn't dare bob it! It is really in 1926 when that look started to come in. There *were* some people doing it before that, but they were very brave, very avant-garde.' And not living under Lord Grantham's roof.

In fact, so rebellious was the act of cutting off one's hair that in 1920 F. Scott Fitzgerald had written a short story, 'Bernice Bobs Her Hair', which explored the furore one such young lady caused by doing so.

Re-creating this look is not easy to do on your own hair, although many women did, and there are no short-cuts to following in Marcel's footsteps, warns Vaughan. 'He created the wave to look like natural curly hair – S-shapes,' she says. 'You take the tong, twist it up and push it in one direction and the hair in the other. So then you get that wave. Then you pull the tong out and you go in the other direction. It is quite technical, but there is a rhythm to it once you get it.'

In the *Downton* trailers the team use modern hair tongs instead, as safety must win out over authenticity. 'The women of the time would have used tongs that they put in the oven, but they could often burn, so we're not going quite that authentic; it's too risky. We can get the same look by using electric tongs – and these women were using electric ones by the end of the Marcel era as well,' says Vaughan.

She also uses false hair to create the period style. 'I want the look,' Vaughan continues. 'But you have to consider the amount of time it takes to achieve it, and the maintenance of it on set. You don't want to put all that product on people's hair, so instead you can use a wig.'

KEEPING IT IN THE FAMILY

The Marcel wave appears not only on the heads of the younger generation in series four, but also on those of the fashionable older members of the family. To get the look right, the team plastered the walls of the make-up trailer with pages from a period handbook, *The Art and Craft of Hairdressing*, as well as contemporary images of the style.

SHORT-CUT TO STYLE

To re-create the Marcel wave on just one head of hair can take between 40 minutes to one hour, and involves a lot of styling products. For speed and to spare the actresses' hair, many of the cast wear wigs that have been shaped and coiffed the day before filming. These are kept under nets until the actresses need them, when they can be fitted and finessed quickly and without fuss.

Ladies' Maids and the Art of Hairdressing

The Marcel wave quickly became a favourite of the fashionable smart set in the Twenties. In 1922 *The New York Times* marked the fiftieth anniversary of the style ('one which every woman will appreciate') with a special report describing how the coiffeurs of France planned a thanksgiving week, complete with 'competitions, expositions, balls and banquets' to celebrate the great man. A cynic might suggest that Marcel's popularity with his colleagues was due in no small part to the fact that few women could 'Marcel' their own hair and so many had to pay someone to do it.

This is indeed a key point that the make-up department had to consider, too – who would have been styling each character's hair in their everyday life? Lady Grantham, Mary, Edith and Rose all had the help of a lady's maid, which would have had a strong influence on how good they looked and whether they tried any of these new, tricky styles. Thus it was vitally important that servants like Anna were apprised of the latest looks and, more importantly, how to re-create them.

Formal Styling

Different occasions demand different hairstyles for the ladies, which is another consideration for the make-up team. 'When you're at Highclere it gets really interesting, because everybody is either having dinner, or at a party, or something is happening where they need to have a more formal look,' says Katie Pickles, one of the hair and make-up artists. To create the various up-dos that this look demands, Vaughan and her team switch between using the cast's natural hair, helped by hairpieces to give length or weight, and full-on wigs.

Dressing these elegant hairstyles is also an important part of styling for evening scenes. Jewels, feathers and bandeaux are all crucial to the Twenties party look – and of course tiaras, should you be so lucky. 'People wore hair ornaments in the evening much more than they

do now,' says Caroline McCall. 'If you were a married woman you could wear a tiara, but not if you were unmarried. The aristocracy wore real jewellery, too, but those who couldn't afford genuine gemstones would wear imitation stones made from glass, known as paste.'

Post-war, ladies began to wear tiaras in a modern way, echoing the style of the more democratic bandeau. 'The bandeau originated with Paul Poiret, the French fashion designer in the Teens, who created the sort of clothes Sybil was wearing in the first series,' says McCall. 'People began to pick this up and you started to see pictures of women wearing tiaras in a more fashionable way, set lower on the forehead.' The hair had to complement these decorations and would be sculpted to hide the unsightly 'arms' of the tiaras.

Perfect Partings for the Party Set

For scenes involving many extras, such as parties and club scenes, the six-strong hair and make-up team must call on additional 'dailies' to help them transform the crowd. For instance, when filming busy scenes at the Criterion restaurant in London an extra ten or so hair and make-up artists were on set.

As is typical of the early Twenties' look, the extras wear their hair up and waved, finished with a bandeau or other delicate headpiece.

Adam James Phillips, the show's key hair stylist, admits these styles are kept in place during long filming sessions only with the aid of 'a lot of strategically placed pins and a lot of hairspray'.

For this style the team must first put the hair of each actress in heated rollers to give it volume and some 'bends' to work with, Phillips explains. 'So then when you brush it through you get a much looser wave, but the hair will be going in the right direction. Then you clamp the wave with tongs to accentuate it and add the crests onto the waves.' Elegance personified.

Ugly Duckling to Elegant Swan

What Mary has, Edith tends to want, which in part explains how the latest hairstyle may have spread through the house. 'In my mind, one of the sisters would say, "Oh, I like your hair, can I have that?"' says Vaughan. 'And then Anna did Edith's hair for a little while, because Edith didn't have her own maid. So that's when that journey started. And then their mother might say, "Oh, can you do something similar with mine?" So it evolves like that.'

Laura Carmichael believes that her character's changing style has been partly driven by her attempts to get Sir Anthony Strallan's attention. Although he jilted her at the altar, he did at least notice she had done 'something jolly' to her hair, she laughs.

To the untrained eye, Edith's latest look appears to be a Marcel, but it is in fact another style – finger-waving. Here, soaking wet hair is clamped into waves, then left to dry. 'The hair then lies that bit closer to the head, which suits Laura better,' says Adam James Phillips.

THOROUGHLY MODERN EDITH

Lady Edith in series four is almost unrecognisable from the slightly dowdy, demure-looking daughter we met in the first episodes. The change in her hair to a sleeker, more sophisticated and thoroughly modern style reflects her new attitude to the changing world and how she, as a woman, is embracing these developments.

'It's wonderful to see Lady Edith coming into her own sexuality. She's blooming. She's been seduced by London. I know Laura as an actress enjoyed that element, too – breaking out of what we've come to expect from her so far.'

Charles Edwards

MICHAEL GREGSON

The Generation Gap

While the younger generations at Downton Abbey begin to embrace the changing fashions of the post-war era, others remain immovable in their style. Violet is one such character who steadfastly ignores the winds of change in many ways – including her hair-do. As would most grandmothers, Violet maintains a completely different look to the younger generation, 'more Queen Mary-ish', Vaughan describes it.

'With the older generation, their look is always a couple of years behind. Maybe with the influence of the current hairstyle, but not so up to date,' explains Adam James Phillips. 'I changed Violet's hair a bit this year, so she's still got the piled-up Edwardian look, but it's got more of a Marcel-looking tong to it. The influence would have come in, but just in a different form.'

Conscious that Isobel Crawley does not have a lady's maid in series four, the team have taken a simple approach to her hair. She has not let herself go, though; grieving as she is, she still has her pride. 'Isobel doesn't like to be at a disadvantage,' says Penelope Wilton. 'She's up to the moment, but she dresses her age. She doesn't have her hair in the latest look, but she does what she can with what she's got.'

For the make-up team, the contrasts between the Downton women help to create a visual richness for the viewer. 'Violet is always going to be of another generation – and I love that she is,' says Katie Pickles. 'To see the difference between her and her granddaughters is nice. From a hair and make-up point of view, I love seeing this variance when they are all sitting together.'

Men in
the Chair

The male actors may not need as much finessing as their female counterparts, but they are not ignored by the make-up team. Their lack of hairpieces or wigs and minimal make-up base make the men's pre-filming preparation a much faster process – just 10 to 20 minutes each, 'depending on how much we gossip', says Katie Pickles.

Most have their hair simply slicked over, with the parting on the left (part it the other way and you might have given rise to talk, warn the make-up team). Still, as with the women, there is variation, so that the younger generation look slightly freer at times.

As Carson, Jim Carter likes his hair 'to be immaculate, with the parting dead straight', as befits such a perfectionist, while his underlings may be less rigid. 'Carson would never have a hair out of place, whereas Jimmy is a bit of a rogue so it's nice to have some hair around the face,' says Vaughan. 'It's not slicked right back – it goes across and then it can sometimes flop forward.'

SLICK AND SLEEK

'Facial hair was for the older generation; the younger generation was clean-shaven,' says Magi Vaughan. Stubble was not an option. 'To be unshaven was an absolute no-no; it made you look like a tramp!' The men's hairstyles are quite simple and unfussy, although in series four Robert has been given a little wave through his tresses to reflect the softer styling of the ladies' hair.

STANDARD BEARER

As butler, Carson sets the standard for the staff in many ways – even as far as how the footmen should wear their hair, demanding a smart, well-kept appearance. Tom Branson, now living above stairs, wears his hair either slicked back or in a more natural style, but the biggest change is that we are seeing a lot more of it since he has said goodbye to his chauffeur's cap!

Flower of Scotland

Series three saw the Crawleys'
cousin, Lady Rose, join the family
at Downton Abbey. Under the
protective and very proper wing
of the family, her hair, like her
behaviour, has been tamed – her
wild, tousled mane has become
a sleek wave. She has 'been
Downton-ed', says Magi Vaughan.
'She came from the Scottish
Highlands, so she was quite wild,
but now she's much calmer, much
tamer' – in appearance, at least.

It is a very different look for Lily
James, who plays Rose. Her hair
is naturally dark, but it was dyed a
lighter shade for her part. 'When
Rose was in Scotland and London,
she didn't have much guidance,'
she says. 'Now she is living at
Downton, with a more stable base,
she's trying to behave better, which
is reflected in her hairstyle.'

That said, James admits to a
fondness for wild Rose as she was.
'She has quite a severe look now.
I preferred it when it was free-
flowing,' she says. 'The make-up
is very natural, too. I can't wait
until we move into a time when
we can be bolder!'

STYLE BELOW STAIRS

'There's a bit of a wave in the hair below stairs, too, as if they're practising on each other – Anna's has more happening, and so has the new maid Edna's, because she claims she's been on a

hairdressing course and she has big ambitions,' says Vaughan. 'The style is not as intricate as that of the ladies above stairs, but it's definitely got a wave in it.'

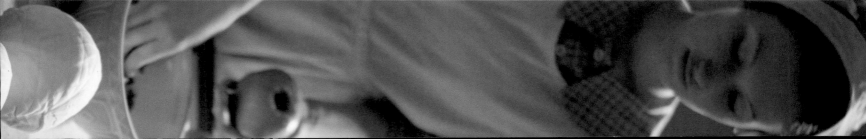

SCRUBBING UP

The biggest change in Daisy's appearance has been that she has scrubbed up more than when she was a lowly kitchen maid. 'I don't have much make-up, they just put a base on, and

I have a bit of a hairpiece in the back because I don't have very long hair. It's not glam! But at least I don't do that greasy hair any more,' says Sophie McShera.

Tricks of the Trade

The rule on set is that actresses must wear 'total sunblock' in order that they all maintain a pale Twenties complexion, says Vaughan. Keeping a tan at bay means she needs to apply only a light touch with make-up. After airbrushing with foundation, Vaughan adds shades of pink for blush and taupe for contouring. The powder blush that was available in the Twenties was a much less convincing cerise, which when worn by Ivy provoked Mrs Patmore's ire!

Natural-looking shades are used to make the eyes 'pop'. 'When you are working in high definition things can go a bit flat, so you want to bring dimension into it,' says Vaughan.

There is also a nod to the youthful shapes that were popular at the time. 'In this period everything was rounded: the eyes, the rouge and the lips, too. All I do, because I don't want them to wear lipstick, is work with a light lip pencil, and just draw some shape on the top of the lip. Just a hint of colour there marries the face into that popular Twenties look.'

'Edith wore the Marcel wave last season, but now she has a finger wave. She is going for a more modern look than Mary; her hair is more elaborate because she tries that little bit harder with it.'

Adam James Phillips
KEY HAIR STYLIST

Insider Knowledge

Downton Diction

Although the show requires the cast to immerse themselves in the era, drama takes precedence over historically accurate diction. 'We decided not to get the people above stairs speaking as they did in the 1920s, because they spoke in a very particular way,' says Alastair Bruce, historical advisor. 'It would have been much more pronounced. So we've tried to make sure that those who live above stairs sound like they might live above stairs in a big house today, and that those below stairs should retain their regional accents.'

For Jim Carter (Mr Carson) it is a case of building on his natural northern accent. 'I just have to make sure it's proper and well enunciated,' he says, 'I use my own voice and posh it up above stairs.' Rob James-Collier does something similar with Thomas. 'I do a "telephone voice" – when anybody picks up the telephone, you'll notice the diction becomes smoother. Above stairs, you see him doing that and then below stairs he slips a bit. He's putting on a show.'

Manners and Social Mores

How people carry themselves has changed greatly since the early twentieth century. 'They were very postured,' reveals Alastair Bruce. 'I make people march and carry things on the axis of their spine, and instantly their shoulders go back.'

There are other rules, too. Above stairs, the servants cannot lean on the furniture or on the walls. As MyAnna Buring (Edna) puts it, 'It's about where you stand and how you move. It really affects you.' Michelle Dockery (Mary) agrees: 'We are always reminded of how we must present ourselves, how we should move and how we must eat at the dinner table – and it definitely influences you in your daily life. I remember someone commenting to Laura [Carmichael] and me when we

were out for dinner one night that we were sitting with our hands off the table, as we had been taught to do.'

It wasn't only the aristocracy who adhered to strict table manners. 'The servants would come in for dinner, on time; they would stand while Mr Carson said grace, then they'd sit down and eat,' says Bruce. He explains that 'after grace is said, the table becomes the Lord's table and is treated with respect; you don't lean on it and you put your hands in your lap when you're not eating.'

Dancing was also more formal in the Twenties. 'We had lots of dancing lessons: one-step, two-step, tango and some Scottish dancing,' says Lily James (Rose). 'The dancing is so different from what has been seen before, revealing how times are moving on in the show.'

MARKING THE MOVES

Filming dance scenes requires some creativity, as playing music on set would ruin the sound. 'We couldn't wear earpieces, because you would see them in our ears,' Lily James remembers of one scene. 'So we were all dancing around in silence!'

Life Mirrors Art?

For the actors, the lines between their lives and those of their characters are not always clear-cut. Like Cora, Elizabeth McGovern is an American mother with English daughters. 'When you raise your children in a country in which you didn't grow up, you have a different frame of reference,' she explains. 'I think Cora looks at her daughters as I look at mine – with awe. They have a little bit of mystery.'

Mrs Hughes, meanwhile, owes her nationality to the actress playing her, Phyllis Logan. 'She was not written as Scottish, but it was decided that was how I would play her,' she remembers. 'It was nice to reach into my background for a sort of general Scottish psyche.' It has helped to shape the Mrs Hughes we see on screen, she thinks. 'She's not an outsider but certainly she's not, for example, a royalist. She's more democratic.'

Some actors are very different to their roles. 'Brendan [Coyle] is the complete opposite,' says Joanne Froggatt. 'He's hilarious. I love Bates, but Brendan is much more fun-loving.'

Chemistry and Camaraderie

For much of the cast the fourth series marks as many years of working together, and so they have developed their own rhythms on set. Hugh Bonneville and Elizabeth McGovern, as Lord and Lady Grantham, have something of the ease of an old married couple – perhaps helped by having worked together previously on a BBC sitcom, *Freezing*. 'I have always had a really easy acting relationship with Hugh,' says McGovern. Her on-screen husband agrees that they are in sync. 'We have our own little ways of getting on with things,' says Bonneville, 'but we can be very direct with each other if something's not clicking. She's completely adorable, and just so easy to work with.'

It is a sentiment echoed by all the cast regarding their colleagues – but most speak particularly warmly of working with Maggie Smith, an icon of the screen. 'We have a very nice time,' says Penelope Wilton (Isobel). 'Maggie, like myself, grew up in theatre. I have always been an enormous admirer, so it's a great joy to be working with her.'

Working Together and Playing Together

Many of the friendships that appear on screen exist off camera, too, fostered by long hours working together. Michelle Dockery and Laura Carmichael play sisters who have a prickly relationship, but they have a much easier friendship in real life.

'We all get on really well, but Michelle and I are very close,' says Carmichael. 'We've bought flats near to each other! Whenever there's a scene together, we get the giggles as we walk into the house as it's such a treat. It was the same with Jess [Brown Findlay, who played Sybil]. We started together and went through a very similar experience. Michelle, for Jess and me, was like a big sister. It was my first job and Michelle was the one who had the experience. We really did look to her for advice and comfort.'

It is a similar story with rival footmen Ed Speleers (Jimmy) and Matt Milne (Alfred). They compete for status when the cameras are rolling, but off set they plan holidays together. 'Everyone's lovely, but Matt and I are particularly close. We both love our football – and we're together a lot, serving together,' says Speleers. Lesley Nicol and Phyllis Logan – otherwise known as Mrs Patmore and Mrs Hughes – have become rather a double act. 'We do have a laugh,' says Nicol. 'She remembers the words of every song ever written. I bop around in the background.'

The house's dividing lines do not hold off screen. 'I have friends above and below stairs,' says Penelope Wilton. 'It's a unique group, because we get on extremely well without getting in each other's pockets.'

'We're very much a family because we've spent so much time together over the years. The feeling on set is very happy – there is something about being a part of something that has become such a success. It's a wonderful atmosphere.'

Michelle Dockery
LADY MARY

The Waiting Game

For actors, filming can involve a lot of waiting for their moment in front of the cameras. For Matt Milne, 'up at Highclere, it's very chilled, and it's mostly downtime. There might be one scene to do at the end of the day, and there might not be a huge amount of preparation for it. So while you are waiting you can just hang out, watch films, read or do whatever you want to do.'

'There is a lot of sitting around, and we do a lot of chatting,' says Laura Carmichael. 'Often, I will bring in a book or newspaper but will barely look at it as someone's always telling a funny story. The other day I was showing lots of silly pictures to Maggie Smith on my iPhone, of cats doing ridiculous things. So that's quite fun.'

The above-stairs cast are particularly fond of games to pass the time. 'We started playing Bananagrams, which is a bit like Scrabble, but without the board,' says Michelle Dockery. 'It's really good fun, and it kind of keeps your brain active between set-ups.'

The Show to Launch a Thousand Careers …

'We really do have a wonderful group of actors,' says Julian Fellowes, 'from a wide variety of backgrounds, often in complete contrast to the part they are playing, and that can be illuminating for me. We also represent every kind of career, from the highly respected and long established to the beginner. Laura Carmichael, for example, had only just left drama school and was working as a doctor's receptionist when she was cast as Edith. Weeks later, she was playing scenes with Maggie Smith. Really it's a sort of fairy tale.'

Carmichael is not the only fresh-faced actress in the show; Cara Theobold (Ivy) was also lucky enough to start her acting career on *Downton Abbey*. 'I left drama school early to do this – my first TV job,' she says. 'It's a brilliant environment for me to learn my craft.'

Also among the cast are experienced actors who had not yet achieved the global fame that *Downton* has given them. 'There are actors who have slaved before the master for many a year,' notes Fellowes. 'Like Lesley Nicol, who I think is one of the best characters in the show. She had been in hits like *East Is East*, but finally she's rung the bell and now has jobs in Hollywood and guests on American television.'

The show has been fortunate in casting some well-known names but, as Fellowes explains, a balance must be maintained. 'If you have too many stars, you can compromise the credibility of the characters. Shirley MacLaine is returning in series four. For that character [Martha Levinson] to work, we needed someone of the calibre of Maggie [Smith], a heavyweight in screen terms.'

'When you're in a scene with Maggie, you just light the touch paper and retire ... She's one of the most cherished actors in the world. She has the quickest, sharpest mind you could ever hope to work with. Acidly funny, but with enormous goodwill underneath.'

Hugh Bonneville
ROBERT, EARL OF GRANTHAM

Trips and Tricks

There's something particularly funny about things going wrong in front of a camera, leaving the cast unable to keep a straight face. 'Oh, it happens endlessly,' says Penelope Wilton. 'You try not to, but when things go wrong, it always makes you laugh.'

The below-stairs cast in particular have had to learn to dash about with loaded trays – and not always with total success. 'Once I had to walk into a scene for background and I dropped my tray. Piccalilli went over everything,' remembers Sophie McShera.

She is not alone. 'On my first week I was carrying a tray full of silver and china,' says Ed Speleers. 'I was striding down the servants' hall and slipped. The whole tray went everywhere.'

Some comic moments are more intentional, he adds. 'There was a sombre moment in a scene when one of the characters gets up and storms out. Rob [James-Collier] thought it would be hilarious in rehearsal to throw himself onto the floor. He's the on-set joker, but he knows when to focus, too.'

Downton's Extended Family

They say never work with children or animals, but as the lives of the characters change from one series to another, increasingly the actors must do both.

Isis, Robert's faithful yellow Labrador, is played by an easy-going seven-year-old called Abbie in series four. Brought in by handlers used to working on films, she is trained to follow actors, although she does need rehearsals – and dog treats – to perform at her best.

She has a particular fan in Allen Leech (Branson), who has to be reminded not to give her too much attention, otherwise the audience would see Robert's dog always trotting after his son-in-law.

The roles of Sybil's daughter, Sybbie, named after her mother, and Mary's son George are currently filled by three children: a little girl called Ava Mann plays Sybbie in the fourth series, while identical twins Logan and Cole Weston play her younger cousin. Casting twin babies is common, as it means reducing the time each individual child has to be present for filming.

Concessions have to be made because of the age of the actors, though. Jim Carter says he might have played Mr Carson as being more at a loss when handling a crying Sybbie in the third series, but wisely he tempered his reaction. 'Carson's a crusty old bachelor, but he would probably have a grandfatherly interest in the kids,' he says. 'I would have liked to have been able to treat the baby like an alien, but that would have freaked her out, so I had to be very affectionate!'

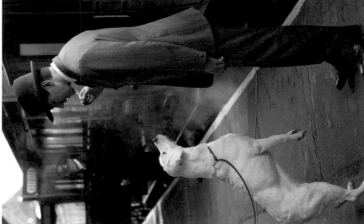

'With children, you'll shoot something, and maybe one day it won't work, then the next time they're in they'll be amazing – they're really unpredictable! It's nice to have kids around. The actors love it.'

Danielle Bennett
SECOND ASSISTANT DIRECTOR

The *Downton Abbey*
Legacy

The *Downton Abbey* Legacy

Downton Abbey's success was not a slow burner once it hit the television screens. The initial overnight audience figure came in at 7.6 million for its Sunday-night debut on ITV in September 2010.

'I was in a meeting about another project, just getting on with my Monday-morning work, and somebody came in with the ratings on a piece of paper, saying – "It's huge,"' remembers Gareth Neame, executive producer. 'That was a really good figure, and it was higher than we were expecting, so we were delighted.'

The big surprise was yet to come. The following Monday, Neame flew to Cannes for the industry event Mipcom, to sell the show overseas, and as he stepped off the plane he immediately got a call from Laura Mackie, then head of drama at ITV. 'She said, "Have you seen the ratings? They are extraordinary."'

The overnight number for the show's second episode had come in even bigger still, he learned, at 8.3 million.

'I walked off the plane and I stood on the runway, waiting for Julian; I was so excited. He was one of the last people to come off the plane, and I said, "I've just got the ratings – it's a huge hit!"'

Gareth Neame
EXECUTIVE PRODUCER

(which include viewing figures for audiences watching the show both live and on playback) were a staggering 9.2 million for episode one and 10 million for episode two, confirming *Downton Abbey* as an immediate hit.

By coincidence, Julian Fellowes was on the same flight, heading to Cannes for meetings about another show, Neame remembers. 'I walked off the plane and I stood on the runway, waiting for Julian; I was so excited. He was one of the last people to come off the plane, and I said, "I've just got the ratings – it's a huge hit!"'

The critics, meanwhile, were as warm in their support as the audience. *Downton* holds a Guinness World Record for the highest critical review ratings for a

'It was pretty much unheard of in my experience. With most shows, you start high, then have a dip by the second week as a certain number of viewers will not come back. I had never seen a show go up so substantially between weeks one and two.'

In fact, the consolidated ratings

a TV show, after its first series scored 92 out of 100 on Metacritic (a site that aggregates reviews), making it the highest-scoring reviewer-rated show ever.

Amid the buzz, the show began to percolate in the public's consciousness very quickly. The Saturday before the second episode aired in the UK, Neame heard a guest on Radio 4 add the caveat of 'I don't mean that in a *Downton Abbey* kind of way.' 'One episode had played and somebody was using it as a touchstone for something completely unrelated,' he remarks.

The cast, as the faces of the show, were beginning to sense success in a more direct way. Lesley Nicol (Mrs Patmore) noticed that when her fellow dog-walkers greeted her they were rather 'more bubbly and giggly' than usual. The wake-up moment for Phyllis Logan (Mrs Hughes), meanwhile, came when a London radio DJ started a men's fan club for the show, dubbed 'Manton Abbey'. 'When all these ruffy-tuffy booted men were joining, I thought, "Oh, this is bizarre!" I am surprised it appeals to men, because I would see it more as a woman's sort of thing, really. But it seems to have touched all manner of people.'

And then the Granthams went global. After its UK debut the show began to air around the world, notably in January 2011 when it had its US premiere on PBS, the non-profit public broadcasting television network. *Downton Abbey* was starting to generate a buzz overseas.

Later the same year, the second series aired in the UK to even bigger numbers, helped by word of mouth and, specifically, the 'will they, won't they?' speculation around Mary and Matthew's relationship.

> **'When I see what's on TV in America I'm struck by how deeply cynical it is. Maybe Americans are relieved to watch a show in which there's a basic decency to most of the people. They seem to find that refreshing.'**
>
> **Elizabeth McGovern**
> CORA, COUNTESS OF GRANTHAM

There was some inevitable backlash to the show's success, Neame remembers. 'People were saying, "It's moving too quickly through history," the episodes are too fast-paced, we can't keep up with them."' Yet it was clear to him that these very elements were thrilling others. 'By the second series, critics and viewers were more conscious of the kind of drama we are making, which is a contemporary family relationship saga,' he says. 'Those who complained about it being fast-paced were the traditional parts of the audience. But the fact that it *was* fast-paced was why we were getting kids in America watching the show.'

And they continue to watch. *Downton* became and continues to be PBS's highest-rating drama in its more than 40-year history. The shocking series-three finale pulled in more than 12 million viewers, beating all its prime-time rivals in that one night.

Of course, it is not just the kids who are watching the show in the US. When Hillary Clinton stepped down as US Secretary of State, the cast made a tape for her, remembers Neame. 'When it was played at her celebration dinner, Bill Clinton turned to the British Ambassador and said, "This really is her favourite show."'

For Elizabeth McGovern (Cora), *Downton*'s Stateside success has been particularly sweet. 'It was nice for me to go back home with a sense of pride in being part of the show; I felt I could hold my head up high – just like all the other members of the cast.'

She has her own thoughts on why her home country has so embraced the series. 'When I see what's on TV in America, I'm struck by how deeply cynical it is,' she

says, 'Maybe Americans are relieved to watch a show in which there's a basic decency to most of the people – not that everybody on the show is perfect. They seem to find that refreshing, along with the fact that it is a very nice escape and very pretty to look at.'

Of course, America is only part of the story. *Downton* now airs in 200-plus territories, so the Crawleys and their servants are familiar to an estimated 120 million people around the world.

Jim Carter (Mr Carson) experienced his own 'Dr Livingstone, I presume?' moment on a cycling holiday. 'I was in my Lycra gear, sweating like a horse, walking through temples in the Cambodian jungle,' he remembers. He was far from the world of the Abbey, but when spotted by a group of Chinese tourists, he heard a familiar cry: 'Oh, Mr Carson!'

It is an experience likely to be repeated many times over, as networks around the world transmit the show to enthusiastic viewers. Their reasoning for taking on the show varied. In Germany, executives at public broadcaster ZDF believed *Downton* would be embraced by an audience known to love stories about the aristocracy. At Spain's Antena 3, management looked to the long tradition of British dramas finding favour there, particularly *Upstairs, Downstairs*. Brazil's Globosat, meanwhile, having seen the show's success with its UK and US audiences, took the gamble of airing the series in a slot normally kept for contemporary drama – it paid off. *Downton* is a hit around the world – and the show's reach is still growing. Indeed, a recent deal with CCTV in China means it will be dubbed into Mandarin for a potential audience of 100 million.

So why does the show translate so easily into other countries and other cultures? Neame has his own theory on how the Abbey's inhabitants are viewed. 'It sounds absurd in a way when I say it, but I think audiences around the world look at that group of people as an extension of their family,' he says. 'That's the soap-opera element. It happened with *Dallas*. I just hope that we bring something literary to the screen that has a beautiful production value. Essentially the dramatic and narrative tricks are very similar, though.'

Downton's international momentum has been helped by its award successes, thinks Neame. While the first series performed well in the US, it still represented a small slice of America's vast, saturated TV market. Then came the 2011 Emmys. 'We sent screeners of the show out to all the Academy members – and there are many thousands of them. It was the only way to make sure that people voting had seen the show,' he says. 'The awards drive the business, because the more people are made familiar with the show, the more people will watch it.'

The mass mail-out worked. The show picked up six Emmy Awards, prompting reports of '*Downton* sweeps the board' back home. 'The show just came out of nowhere from England and all of a sudden was on this world stage, competing with the top shows in the US,' says Joanne Froggatt (Anna). 'That was very exciting. The American side has been the happy surprise for a lot of us. They are used to doing productions with very high budgets and production values. It's great that something from the UK has been able to compete.'

But *Downton*'s critical success did not end there. Today, with a total of 27 Emmy nominations, it is the most nominated non-American show in Emmy history, and has added two Golden Globes to its awards cabinet.

The show also claimed victory over US heavyweights *Mad Men* and *Homeland*, among others, for a Screen Actors Guild (SAG) Award in early 2013. This was an event that was particularly memorable for Michelle Dockery. 'That award was so special, because it's an ensemble award [for best ensemble in a drama], and that says so much about the show,' she says. 'We really weren't expecting to win, being up against such incredible shows. It was just the most amazing night.'

Not all the cast members were present, due to filming commitments. But those who did attend nominated Phyllis Logan (Mrs Hughes) to give a speech if they won. Assuming the award would go to *Mad Men*, she ended up having to improvise on the podium.

As well as enjoying formal recognition by the industry, the show is celebrated by its millions of fans in the most creative of ways. Most period dramas aren't spoofed by P. Diddy, but then most period dramas are not *Downton Abbey*. The hip-hop star proclaimed himself an 'Abbeyhead' in a video in which he was superimposed into scenes from the series. *The Simpsons* have also paid tribute to *Downton Abbey* in their opening-sequence spoof *Simpton Abbey*.

The show has become a cultural touchstone, and something to play with, too. On the internet there can be found scores of YouTube compilations made by fans – romantic shots of Mary and Matthew or Bates and Anna set to music, vying for popularity with Violet's acid one-liners. There are also numerous parodies and re-enactments that have been created by big-name stars.

The show's creators see such tributes as the ultimate compliment. Julian Fellowes loved 'Downton Arby's', a viral short about a fast-food chain with familiar problems. 'It was this pancake house with three daughters … Those things are always flattering, because you've got into the zeitgeist and very few shows do that. Even shows that are pretty popular don't get into that level of spoofery and reference, and that has been good fun.'

Indeed, the cast have, on occasion, played along. Gareth Neame's favourite spoof is 'the one that our actors did themselves – the sort of mash-up of Downton and Breaking Bad for [US show] The Colbert Report'. The resulting 'Breaking Abbey', a period-drama-meets-drug-fuelled-crime-caper, was definitely one to remember: 'Right you are, Mr Carson,' says Thomas the footman. 'Allow me to bring the mobile lab.'

Another benefit of the global success the show has enjoyed is the increasing pull that Downton holds for big-name stars. The great Hollywood actress Shirley stardust on set. Fellowes, for one, planned to visit the set for the appearance in series four by the acclaimed opera singer Dame Kiri Te Kanawa, 'which I was enthralled to see. I think it's rather a high moment for Downton.'

The regular cast themselves are also enjoying boosted profiles around the world – and all that that entails. 'I'm not interested in fame,' says Matt Milne (Alfred), 'but work-wise it does mean that I've been able to do a couple of interesting things I wanted to do.'

Ed Speleers (Jimmy), another more recent addition to the cast, tries not to think too much about the show's success. 'It was a bit of an opportunity for me and I was delighted to get the chance,' he says. 'But if you worry too much about how big the show is, you can't get into the work.'

Still, the attention can be tricky to ignore. Lesley Nicol (Mrs Patmore) remembers a 2012 trip to the theatre with Sophie McShera (Daisy) in New York, which descended into bedlam as the pair were recognised. 'It

'I love having Shirley MacLaine on the set because she's a really engaging, fun person. She brings so much experience and history, and all of that comes with her before she even walks through the door.'

Elizabeth McGovern
CORA, COUNTESS OF GRANTHAM

MacLaine returns in series four as the indomitable Martha, mother to Cora and a worthy match for Violet. 'I love having her on the set, because she's a really engaging, fun person, but also it's just really nice to have another American there because I so understand where she's coming from,' says Elizabeth McGovern. 'She brings so much experience and history, and all of that comes with her before she even walks through the door. That is thrilling.'

The casting of MacLaine was a careful choice, not a case of bringing in some Hollywood razzmatazz for the sake of it – although everyone enjoys a sprinkle of extra was crackers; people shouting, screaming, running after us in the theatre.' She and McShera were, she stresses, 'done up with lots of make-up and looking better than we do in the show!'

Certainly, a lot of the cast think they receive more attention from the public in the US than in the UK, where Jim Carter suspects people are 'a little more reticent to confront them'. Laura Carmichael (Edith) once found on an overseas trip that people can easily confuse the character and the actor when a waiter in a bar was convinced he knew her. He finally twigged who she was and offered her free drinks all night, leaving her musing on the strangeness of a 'young guy from Brooklyn watching an English period drama that has come from ITV'.

A raised profile translates into more opportunities for an actor, with many of the cast now using the six months in which they are not filming to fit in feature films. 'Allen [Leech] has done a picture with John Cusack, Michelle [Dockery] has done a movie with Julianne Moore and Liam Neeson, and Hugh [Bonneville] is doing a big movie with George Clooney and Matt Damon,' says Fellowes, reeling off a few examples. 'The show has had the most extraordinary effect on the movie-making colony. I think it's absolutely great that the cast have been given these opportunities.'

For the crew, too, *Downton* acts as a similar calling card, helped by the many industry awards the show has won. However, the real draw of the job is the audience. 'It's hard work, doing this, and we do it for half the year with very long hours,' says Liz Trubridge. 'But there's nothing like it when you know that people around the world, millions of people, are waiting to see the finished result. That's the sheer pleasure of making this show.'

For some of those behind the camera, the show's growing scale has also meant their jobs have changed in a way that those of the cast have not. 'We started out on this thinking we were making a British TV show that would hopefully go on and sell round the world,' says Neame. 'Now, I'm thinking we're making a series for people round the world, which premieres on ITV. The homeland of the programme is ITV, but it is as big in America as it is here – socially, culturally – and I think it is in many other countries, too.'

For him, the shift has been to move back from the detail of the filming stage to concentrate more on the scripts, casting, editing and post-production – 'the key storytelling moments'. Another aspect of the job which has ballooned is that of managing a global brand. This role did not exist when the show first aired, but now it encompasses working on everything from award

ceremonies, press and marketing to merchandising through clothing and homeware lines.

Meanwhile, the series is also setting the trend for new shows on our screens, but it's a tough act to follow, notes Laura Carmichael. 'In the way that *Mad Men* has its aesthetic, *Downton* has its own period and look – it's so dreamy.'

Yet all good things must come to an end one day, and so it is inevitable that, even at its peak, the storytellers behind the show are always thinking about what will come next. The creators are adamant that they will give *Downton Abbey* the stage exit it deserves. 'Just as we managed the start of the show, I want to manage the end of it in the same way, so that when it finishes, it will hopefully be a perfectly formed piece,' says Neame. 'I want it to get out at the right time, so that when there are no more episodes you can still look back on it five years later and think, "That was perfect as it was."'

That said, fans can sleep easy because the producer feels the show is still growing. There is no end in sight just yet. Could there even be a *Downton* movie, a route other TV hits have followed? 'That's possible,' Neame says. '*Downton* is so loved that we hope it will be watched by audiences for years and years to come.'

Julian Fellowes is likewise hopeful that *Downton Abbey* has carved out a niche in the collective memory. 'What I would like to feel is that we are one of those milestone bits of television that people remember years later – that's enough for me,' says Fellowes. 'I have chosen to make my life painting pictures in the air. You finish them, and people either enjoy them or they don't. But either way, by the next day they're gone – and, you know, I'm okay with that.'

For now, the cast and crew – and the audience who are watching their work – are holding on for the ride. 'We never would have imagined how huge the show would become,' says Michelle Dockery. 'Nothing lasts forever, and the show will end one day, so we're enjoying it while it lasts.'

Series Four Cast List

Actor	Character
Andrew Alexander	Sir John Bullock, Bt.
Samantha Bond	Lady Rosamund Painswick
Hugh Bonneville	Robert, Earl of Grantham
Di Botcher	Nanny West
MyAnna Buring	Edna Braithwaite
Laura Carmichael	Lady Edith Crawley
Gary Carr	Jack Ross
Jim Carter	Charles Carson
Raquel Cassidy	Phyllis Baxter
Paul Copey	Mr Mason
Brendan Coyle	John Bates
Tom Cullen	Viscount Gillingham
Joanna David	The Duchess of Yeovil
Michelle Dockery	Lady Mary Crawley
Kevin Doyle	Mr Molesley
Charles Edwards	Michael Gregson
James Fox	Lord Aysgarth
Joanne Froggatt	Anna Bates
Bernard Gallagher	Bill Molesley
Paul Giamatti	Harold Levinson
Nigel Harman	Mr Green
Nicky Henson	Charles Grigg
Lily James	Lady Rose MacClare
Rob James-Collier	Thomas Barrow
Patrick Kennedy	Terence Sampson
Allen Leech	Tom Branson
Daisy Lewis	Sarah Bunting
Phyllis Logan	Elsie Hughes
Elizabeth McGovern	Cora, Countess of Grantham
Shirley MacLaine	Martha Levinson
Sophie McShera	Daisy Mason
Matt Milne	Alfred Nugent
Lesley Nicol	Beryl Patmore
Julian Ovenden	Charles Blake
Brendan Patricks	Evelyn Napier
Douglas Reith	Lord Merton
David Robb	Dr Clarkson
Andrew Scarborough	Tim Drewe
Maggie Smith	Violet, Dowager Countess of Grantham
Ed Speleers	Jimmy Kent
Jeremy Swift	Mr Spratt
Kiri Te Kanawa	Dame Nellie Melba
Cara Theobold	Ivy Stuart
Harriet Walter	Lady Shackleton
Penelope Wilton	Isobel Crawley

Series Four Crew List

PRODUCERS

Gareth Neame	Executive Producer
Julian Fellowes	Executive Producer
Liz Trubridge	Executive Producer
Nigel Marchant	Co-Executive Producer
Rupert Ryle-Hodges	Producer

DIRECTOR

David Evans	Director (Episodes 1 & 2)
Catherine Morshead	Director (Episodes 3 & 4)
Philip John	Director (Episodes 5 & 6)
Ed Hall	Director (Episodes 7 & 8)
Jon East	Director (Episode 9)

PRODUCTION

Ian Hogan	Line Producer
Oliver Cockerham	Production Coordinator
Joel Stokes	Assistant Coordinator
Jake Cullen	Assistant to Liz Trubridge
Harriet Patton	Production Assistant
Sam Harman	Production Runner

ACCOUNTS DEPARTMENT

Andrew J. Hill	Production Accountant
Jo Sanders	First Assistant Accountant
Matthew Lawson	Payroll Accountant

ADVISORY DEPARTMENT

Alastair Bruce	Historical Advisor
Diana Scrivener	Choreographer

ART DEPARTMENT

Donal Woods	Production Designer
Mark Kebby	Supervising Art Director
Charmian Adams	Art Director
Gina Cromwell	Set Decorator
Sue Morrison	Production Buyer
Laura Conway-Gordon	Standby Art Director
Neil McAllister	Standby Art Director
Chantelle Valentine	Assistant Art Director
Caroline Barton	Art Dept Assistant
Lisa Heathcote	Food Economist
Tara Royston	Petty Cash Buyer

ASSISTANT DIRECTORS

Chris Croucher	First Assistant Director (Episodes 1, 2, 5, 6, 9)
Alex Streeter	First Assistant Director (Episodes 3, 4, 7, 8)
Danielle Bennett	Second Assistant Director
Toby Spanton	Crowd 2nd Assistant Director
Eddie Williams	Third Assistant Director
Charlotte Vaughan	Base Assistant Director

CAMERA DEPARTMENT

Nigel Willoughby	Director of Photography (Episodes 1, 2, 3, 4, 7, 8, 9)
Graham Frake	Director of Photography (Episodes 5, 6)
Ian Clark	A Camera Operator
George Grieve	A Camera Focus Puller
Joanne Smith	A Camera Clapper Loader
John Hembrough	B Camera/Steadicam Operator (Episodes 1, 2, 3, 4, 7, 8)
David Morgan	B Camera/Steadicam Operator (Episodes 5, 6, 9)
Milos Moore	B Camera Focus Puller
Gabriel Albuquerque	B Camera Clapper Loader (Episodes 1, 2, 3, 4, 7, 8, 9)
Rachel Clark	B Camera Clapper Loader (Episodes 5, 6)
Villing Chong	Digital Imaging Technician

CASTING

Jill Trevellick CDG	Original Casting
Dan Hubbard	Casting Director
Gemma Sykes	Casting Associate
Ana Soria	Casting Assistant

CATERING

Bon Appetit	

CONSTRUCTION

Barry Moll	Construction Manager
Nick Wood	Supervising Painter
Roger Wilkins	Carpenter
Joseph Willmott	Carpenter

CONTINUITY

Sarah Garner	Script Supervisor (Episodes 1, 2)
Sam Donovan	Script Supervisor (Episodes 3, 4, 7, 8)
Caroline Holder	Script Supervisor (Episodes 5, 6)
Kerensa Magnusson	Script Supervisor (Episode 9)

COSTUME DEPARTMENT

Caroline McCall	Costume Designer
Heather Leat	Costume Supervisor
Poli Kyriacou	Assistant Costume Designer
Asia Macey	Wardrobe Mistress
Sally Crees	Crowd Wardrobe Mistress
Sarah Humphrey	Cutter
Isabelle Fraser	Standby Costume
Aimee Davis	Standby Costume
Jessica Phillips	Standby Costume

EDITORIAL DEPARTMENT

Al Morrow	Editor (Episodes 1, 2, 5, 6, 8, 9)
Justin Krish	Editor (Episodes 3, 4)
Paul Garrick	Editor (Episode 7)
Dan Crinnion	Assistant Editor

ELECTRICAL DEPARTMENT

Tom Gates	Gaffer
Philip Hurst	Best Boy
Kevin Heatherington	Electrician
Steve Casey	Electrician

FACILITIES

On-Set	

GRIP DEPARTMENT

Simon Fogg	Key Grip
Bobby Williams	B Camera Grip

LOCATIONS DEPARTMENT

Mark 'Sparky' Ellis	Location Manager
John Prendergast	Assistant Location Manager
Tom Barnes	Unit Manager

MAKE UP & HAIR DEPARTMENT

Magi Vaughan	Make-up & Hair Designer
Erika Okvist	Make-up & Hair Supervisor
Adam James Phillips	Key Hair
Katie Pickles	Make-up & Hair Artist
Lorraine Hill	Make-up & Hair Artist

MUSIC

John Lunn	Composer

POST-PRODUCTION DEPARTMENT

Jessica Rundle	Post-Production Supervisor
Nicki Gunning	Post-Production Coordinator
Picture Post	The Farm
Sound Post	Hackenbacker
Titles	Huge Design

PROPS

Charlie Johnson	Prop Master
Tom Pleydell Pearce	Prop Master
Damian Butlin	Standby Propman
Mark Quigley	Standby Propman
Stuart Silver	Dressing Propman
Don Santos	Dressing Propman
Kevin Fleet	Dressing Propman

PUBLICITY DEPARTMENT

Victoria Brooks	Director of Milk Publicity
Una Maguire	Publicity Director
Jessica Morris	Unit Publicist
Nick Briggs	Stills Photographer

SCRIPT

Steve Williams	Script Editor
Sarah Linton	Script Editor

SFX

Mark Holt	SFX Supervisor
Dave Holt	SFX Technician

SOUND DEPARTMENT

Alistair Crocker	Sound Recordist
Rob Saunders	Sound Maintenance Engineer
Matt Loveridge	Sound Assistant/2nd Boom Operator

STANDBY DEPARTMENT

Chris Sibley-Hale	Standby Carpenter
Lee Howarth	Standby Rigger

STUNTS

Tom Lucy	Stunt Coordinator

TRANSPORT

Symon Butcher	Unit Driver
Kevin O'Keeffe	Unit Driver
Pat Coleman	Unit Driver
Erol Halil	Unit Driver

VFX

The Senate Visual Effects

CARNIVAL

Kimberley Hikaka	Head of Production
Zoe Edwards	Production Executive
Nion Hazell	Production Coordinator
Chrissie Broadway	Production Assistant
Clare Hardwick	Legal and Business Affairs
Vickie Cameron	Legal and Business Affairs

HarperCollins*Publishers*
77–85 Fulham Palace Road,
Hammersmith, London W6 8JB

www.harpercollins.co.uk

First published by HarperCollins*Publishers* 2013

10 9 8 7 6 5 4

Text by Emma Rowley © HarperCollins 2013
The author asserts the moral right to be identified as the author of this work
Foreword by Gareth Neame © Gareth Neame 2013

A Carnival Films / Masterpiece Co-Production

Downton Abbey set photography © 2010–2013 Carnival Film & Television Ltd
Downton Abbey Series 1–4 © 2010, 2011, 2012 and 2013
Carnival Film & Television Ltd
Downton Abbey™ and Downton™ Carnival Film & Television Ltd
carnival © 2005 Carnival Film & Television Ltd
Masterpiece is a trademark of the WGBH Educational Foundation

Photography by Nick Briggs
Additional photography by Giles Keyte and Nick Wall
Design by This-Side

A catalogue record of this book is available from the British Library
ISBN 978-0-00-753366-5

Printed and bound in Italy by L.E.G.O. SpA

This book belongs to:

David Walliams

PRESENTS...

THERE'S A SNAKE

Miss Bloat

First published by HarperCollins Children's Books in 2016
HarperCollins Children's Books is a division of HarperCollins Publishers Ltd.
Text © David Walliams 2016. Illustrations © Tony Ross 2016
Cover lettering of author's name © Quentin Blake 2010
David Walliams and Tony Ross assert the moral right to be identified as the
author and illustrator of the work.
A CIP catalogue record for this title is available from the British Library.

1 3 5 7 9 10 8 6 4 2
Printed and bound in Italy
ISBN: 978-0-00-817270-1

The boring bits

IN MY SCHOOL!

Illustrated by the artistic genius
Tony Ross

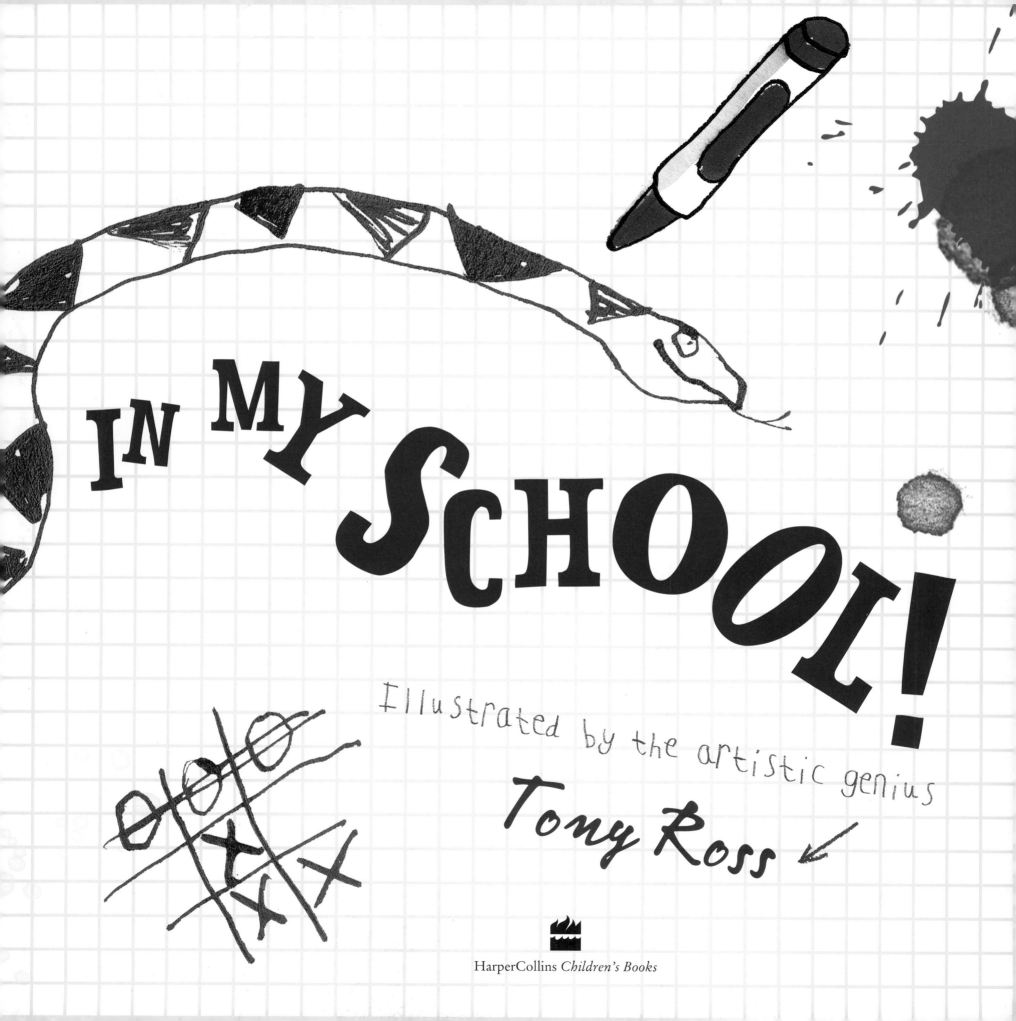

HarperCollins *Children's Books*

David
and
Bert

To the Three Amigos,
Eddie, Frankie
and Alfred.
D.W.

Stanley

Tony

Dorothy

To Ruth, with thanks.
T.R.

I ♥ CATS

Mr Bright had told all the children in his class
it was Bring-your-pet-to-school Day. Everyone
rushed into the playground to meet the animals.
There was…

a *stupidly cute* gerbil,

a **tiny** goldfish,

a **FAT** cat,

a one-hundred-year-old tortoise

and a **tall** dog.

Last to arrive, as usual, was a little girl called Miranda.
She was riding on the back of an **enormous, *slithery snake.***
"Meet Penelope, my pet python!"
announced Miranda.

On seeing the snake the other children screamed,

"Aaarrgh!"

Miranda **loved** being different. She always stood out at school with her

individual take on school uniform,   her cartwheels down the corridors

and her funny answers in class.

A python is a rather unusual pet but Miranda and Penelope had **so much fun** playing together. For the little girl the snake would pretend to be…

a balloon,

a scarf,

a hula-hoop,

a telescope,

a trombone…

and sometimes when they were both feeling particularly mischievous…

a third arm!

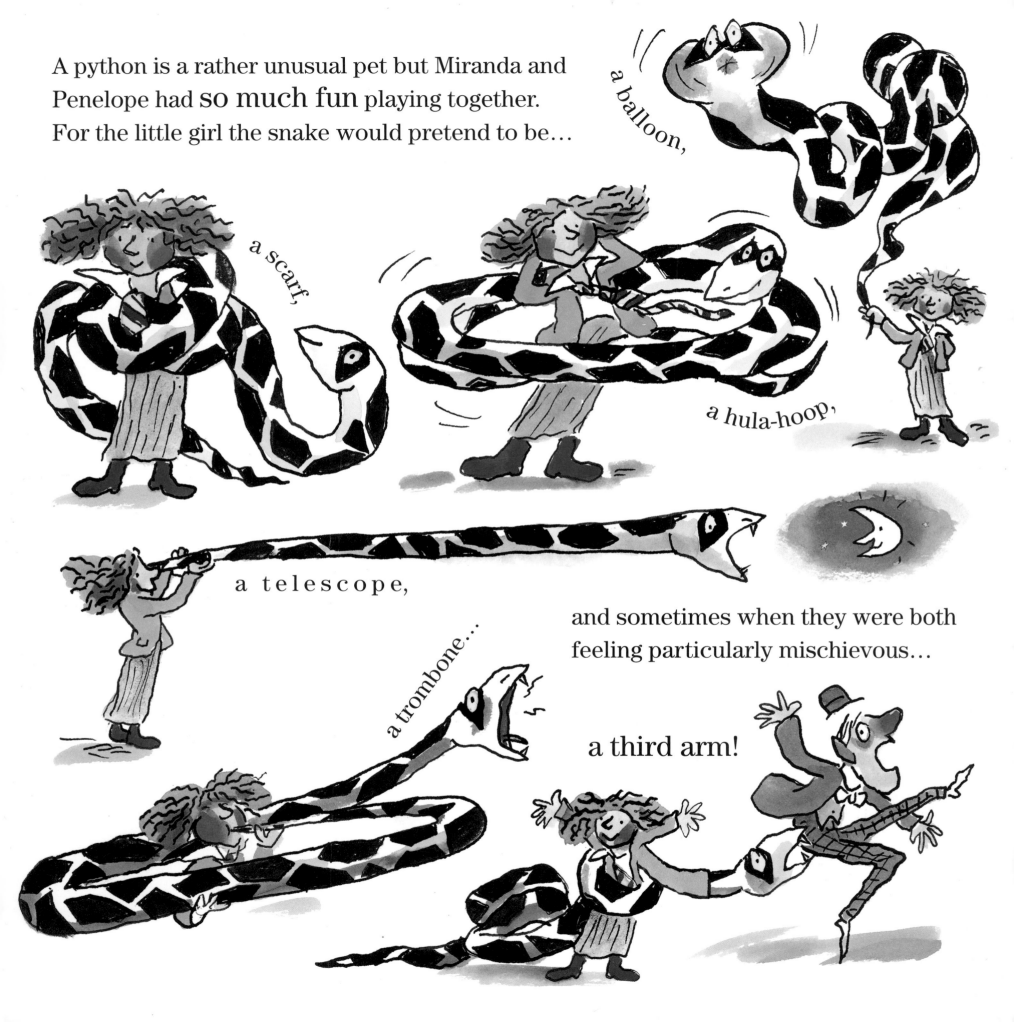

"Come and give her a **tickle**," encouraged Miranda.
But the other children were too scared.
Penelope was a python, after all.
And pythons **EAT** people.
All the pets were frightened too.

The **large** dog
yanked on his lead,
sending his tiny
owner flying.

The **goldfish**
tried to hide
behind **some**
water.

The **tortoise**
made a rather
slooooooooooow run
for it.

The cute **gerbil** flashed her gnashers and didn't look so cute any more.

The **FAT** cat just carried on napping.

Miranda slid down her snake.

The little girl **tickled** her python under the chin, and the snake smiled. "See? She's very friendly."

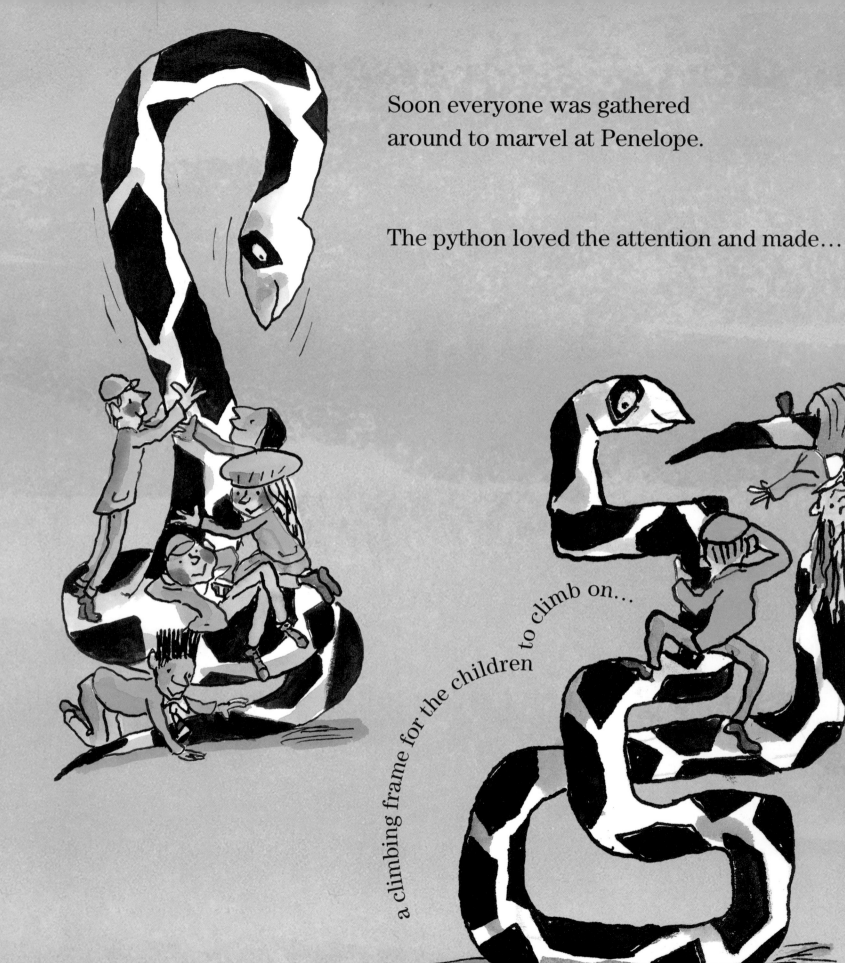

Soon everyone was gathered
around to marvel at Penelope.

The python loved the attention and made...

a climbing frame for the children to climb on...

steps for them to step up…

and a fireman's pole for them to slide back down.

Penelope even helped the children learn their numbers, although she could only go up to 9.

1 + 8 = 9

This was turning into the **best day of school ever.** But then…

Miss Bloat didn't like animals much. Or children.

"It's Bring-your-pet-to-school Day," spluttered Mr Bright.

"And Penelope is my pet," said Miranda.

…as the headmistress stuffed their pets into the
LOST PROPERTY CUPBOARD!

Except for Penelope the snake.
Miss Bloat had other ideas for her…

"This disgusting thing is coming with me," bellowed the headmistress. With that, she dragged the poor python along the corridor to her office. "Where are you going to put Penelope?" asked Miranda.

"In the BIN!"

"Nooooooo!"

Miss Bloat crammed the snake into her bin and **slammed** the lid shut.
Then she plonked herself down on top so the python couldn't
escape. The bin rattled and rattled but…
Penelope was **trapped.**

Downstairs in the classroom, tears rolled down Miranda's cheeks. All the children were sad to have had their pets taken away, but no one was sadder than Miranda. The little girl feared she would never see Penelope again.

At the end of the day Miranda dashed upstairs to Miss Bloat's office to try to make her change her mind.

There was no answer, so slowly Miranda pushed open the door, only to see…

Penelope sitting in the headmistress's chair!

Miranda ran towards her pet and gave her a humongous hug.

Miss Bloat was nowhere to be seen, so the girl grabbed the key on the desk…

ran to the **LOST PROPERTY CUPBOARD** as fast as she could and unlocked it. The animals were overjoyed to be set free.

WHOOOO

Then Miranda and all the pets slid down Penelope's back into the playground.

Penelope entertained everybody again.
She made…

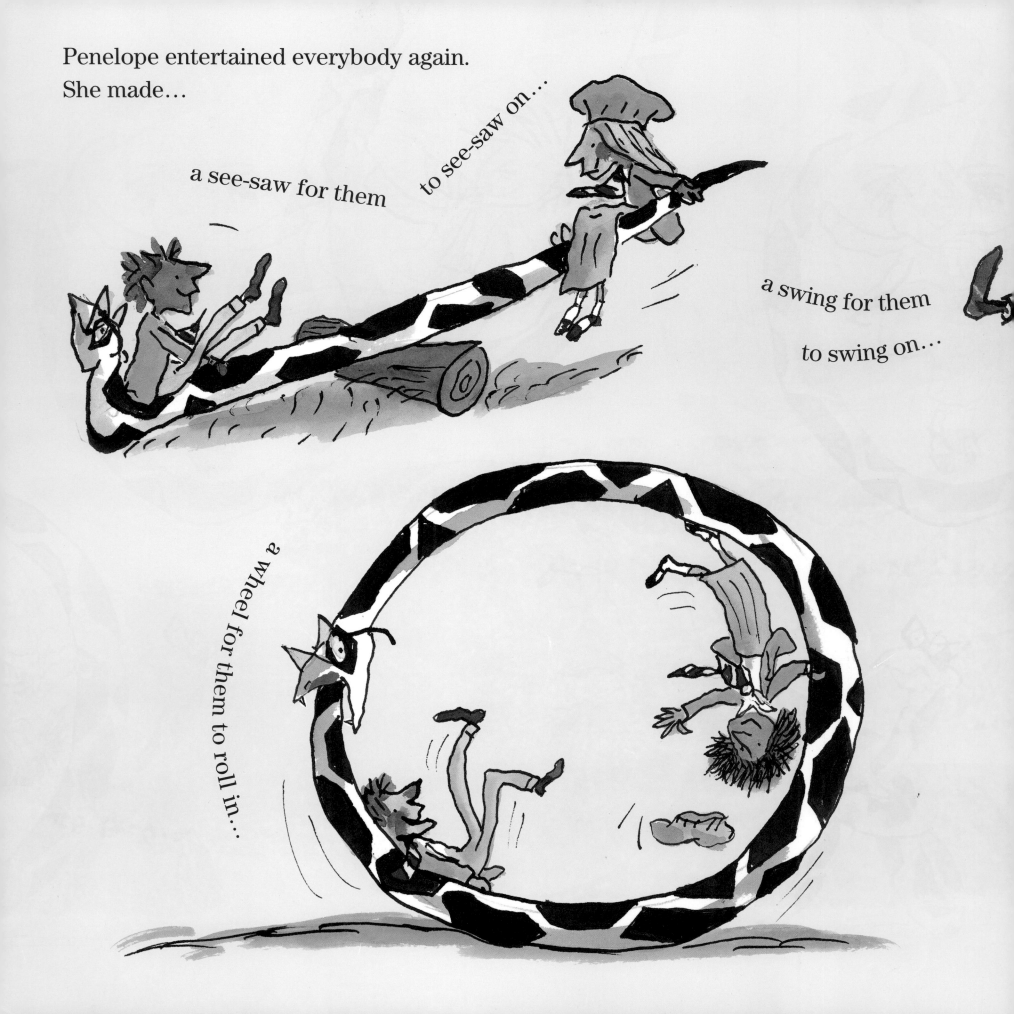

a see-saw for them

to see-saw on…

a swing for them

to swing on…

a wheel for them to roll in…

and a skipping rope to skip with.

Penelope even helped some of the younger children with the alphabet, although it was hard to do an "X".

U V W X Y Z

As for Miss Bloat, she had completely disappeared. So Mr Bright was made headmaster. Now the children were allowed to bring in all their favourite animals whenever they wanted. The school became home to every sort of fantastic creature…

a giraffe,

an ostrich,

a tiger,

a gorilla,

an elephant,

a kangaroo,

a crocodile,

a grizzly bear...

and even a colony of penguins.

But the **STAR ATTRACTION** was always Penelope.

Though Miranda had noticed that there was
something different about her python…

There was a bulge.
A **BIG** bulge in the snake's tummy.
A bulge in the shape of Miss Bloat.
But the little girl thought it best not to say anything.